Kylian Mbappe

Deconstructing the Genius Behind the Goals

(This Article Exposes the Great Waves Mbappe is Making in Soccer)

Arthur Whitlow

Published By **Frank Joseph**

Arthur Whitlow

All Rights Reserved

Kylian Mbappe: Deconstructing the Genius Behind the Goals (This Article Exposes the Great Waves Mbappe is Making in Soccer)

ISBN 978-0-9949842-2-7

No part of this guidebook shall be reproduced in any form without permission in writing from the publisher except in the case of brief quotations embodied in critical articles or reviews.

Legal & Disclaimer

The information contained in this book is not designed to replace or take the place of any form of medicine or professional medical advice. The information in this book has been provided for educational & entertainment purposes only.

The information contained in this book has been compiled from sources deemed reliable, and it is accurate to the best of the Author's knowledge; however, the Author cannot guarantee its accuracy and validity and cannot be held liable for any errors or omissions. Changes are periodically made to this book. You must consult your doctor or get professional medical advice before using any of the suggested remedies, techniques, or information in this book.

Upon using the information contained in this book, you agree to hold harmless the Author from and against any damages, costs, and expenses, including any legal fees potentially resulting from the application of any of the information provided by this guide. This disclaimer applies to any damages or injury caused by the use and application, whether directly or indirectly, of any advice or information presented, whether for breach of contract, tort, negligence, personal injury, criminal intent, or under any other cause of action.

You agree to accept all risks of using the information presented inside this book. You need to consult a professional medical practitioner in order to ensure you are both able and healthy enough to participate in this program.

Table Of Contents

Chapter 1: The Incredible Ascent 1

Chapter 2: A Star Is Born 8

Chapter 3: Breaking Through the Ranks.. 21

Chapter 4: The World Cup Triumph 42

Chapter 5: Joining Paris Saint-Germain ... 53

Chapter 6: Playing Alongside Legends 68

Chapter 7: Style of Play and Skills 80

Chapter 8: Off the Pitch 87

Chapter 9: Challenges and Setback 99

Chapter 10: The Next Generation 109

Chapter 11: Looking Ahead 117

Chapter 12: Early Life and Football Beginnings 128

Chapter 13: Mbappe's Meteoric Rise In As Monaco 142

Chapter 14: Mbappe's Triumph with the French National Team 150

Chapter 15: Mbappe's Transfer to Paris Saint-Germain 158

Chapter 16: Mbappe's Impact on the Football World 166

Chapter 17: Mbappe's Philanthropy and Personal Life... 175

Chapter 1: The Incredible Ascent

A few gamers stand out like blazing stars in the annals of football data, incredible the sport with their brilliance. Kylian Mbappé, whose name has come to stand for electric powered velocity, high-quality expertise, and an unquenchable thirst for triumphing, is taken into consideration in reality one in all them. This soccer prodigy, who's from the Bondy community of Paris, has fast lengthy long past from being a community talent to a global phenomenon.

The movie "The Phenomenal Rise of Kylian Mbappé" transports you on a fascinating journey via the lives and career of this great athlete. Kylian's future modified into set in movement from the instant he grow to be born on December 20, 1998, proper into a football-mad family. He advanced his talents as a teen on Bondy's harsh concrete streets, which served as a haven for undeveloped functionality. Unbeknownst to the area, this quiet more youthful man should cross on to become taken into consideration one of his technology's maximum coveted and famend footballers.

You can have a look at Kylian's brief upward thrust via the degrees of soccer as you switch the pages. He had a activity-changing season with AS Monaco in 2016–2017, captivating both lovers and professionals together together with his super competencies. He become most effective a teenager on the time, however he helped Monaco win the Ligue 1 championship and made an impactful front into the European location.

However, it was in Russia at a few diploma inside the 2018 FIFA World Cup that Kylian Mbappé without a doubt cemented his area in football legend. With his lightning-brief pace, he left defenders in his wake, and his precise finishing obtained him reward and recognize from all around the international. Mbappé changed into an essential trouble of the French national squad and contributed drastically to their 2nd World Cup victory, solidifying his region some of the competition's pinnacle gamers.

The youthful participant proceeded to astonish the footballing international together with his skills, winning important honors just like the Golden Boy and FIFA World Cup Best Young Player. He have emerge as recruited by the usage of the use of Paris Saint-Germain (PSG), who've been aware about his wonderful talent, and this ancient bypass similarly propelled him to superstardom.

Beyond the field, Kylian has captured the hearts of tens of tens of tens of millions along alongside with his charismatic enchantment and humility, transcending soccer and connecting with people everywhere within the worldwide. His humanitarian sports activities sports and determination to charity reasons have set up his popularity as a role version each on and off the field thru using demonstrating a maturity and sensitivity beyond his years.

The tale of "The Phenomenal Rise of Kylian Mbappé" is honestly really one in every of tenacity, strength of mind, and unwavering pressure. It's a celebration of the remarkable heights that can be attained with talent, diligence, and an unwavering dedication to greatness. Join us as we go through the life of Kylian Mbappé, a football phenomenon who has received over fanatics of every age and whose ascent to prominence has been no longer anything short of thoughts-blowing.

1:1 Purpose of the Book

The multifarious objective of the ebook "Kylian Mbappé: A Journey of Excellence" is to provide readers a thorough information of the life and profession of one among football's most terrific game enthusiasts. It seeks to perform the following dreams thru the gripping narrative:

1. Inspire and inspire: The ebook's most important aim is to encourage and encourage readers, mainly bold athletes and younger humans, with the aid of detailing Kylian Mbappé's splendid route. It explores his modest beginnings, perseverance, and difficult art work, demonstrating how he surmounted limitations to grow to be a soccer legend. Readers are inspired with the aid of his narrative and are entreated to pursue their dreams tenaciously.

2. Honor Sports Excellence: Kylian Mbappé has had a extensive impact on the football globe. The e-book highlights his skills, successes, and contributions to the sport as it honors his sports activities prowess. It acknowledges his accomplishments, which incorporates his file-breaking feats, huge awards, and have an effect on on every the French country wide corporation and the clubs he represents.

three. Demonstrate Leadership and Character: In addition to his bodily expertise, Kylian Mbappé's management competencies and individual are highlighted in the e book. It seems at his discipline, sportsmanship, and strength of mind to having a effective have an effect on off the arena. He becomes a feature model for readers to aspire to because of his dedication in social worries and humanitarian paintings, which offer his man or woman size.

four. Provide an Intimate Portrait: The intention of the e book is to offer readers an up-near and personal check Kylian Mbappé. The influences on his person—his formative years, family, and private values—may be higher understood by manner of readers. Readers are drawn in through the personal element of his adventure, which increases the importance and relatability of his triumph.

five. Examine Football's Impact: The e-book explores the game's normal outcomes thru the angle of Kylian Mbappé's career. It talks approximately how the game can unite people from all walks of life and reduce over limitations and cultural variations.

6. Preserve athletic History: Kylian Mbappé is a superb sized individual in present day-day football, and his legacy is a crucial aspect of athletic records. The ebook serves as a record, documenting the specifics of his journey, impact, and accomplishments for present-day soccer fanatics and subsequent generations.

7. Entertainment and Engagement: In addition to being instructive and motivating, the ebook is an specific art work of writing that makes analyzing a delight. It consists of exciting anecdotes, at the back of-the-scenes reminiscences, and professional analyses that keep the reader's interest from starting to give up.

Chapter 2: A Star Is Born

Unassuming Beginnings

The adventure of Kylian Mbappé began out within the peaceful suburbs of Bondy, France. Young Kylian evolved a love for the adorable recreation as he grew up. He have grow to be born on December 20, 1998, to handball movie star Fayza Lamari and previous expert footballer Wilfried Mbappé. His mother and father endorsed him to pursue his aspirations because of the reality they early on located his terrific ability.

Days on the Academy

Kylian joined the community football organization, AS Bondy, while he end up 6 years vintage. Even among more professional gamers, his skills had been apparent, and he fast attracted the attention of scouts from the esteemed Clairefontaine National Football Institute. Kylian delicate his talents and matured proper right into a robust younger skills underneath the course of elite trainers.

Ascending the ranks

After receiving his degree from Clairefontaine, Kylian attracted the interest of numerous prestigious teams in Europe. He ultimately determined to sign up with the kids software program application of AS Monaco in 2013. He made more of a power there along along with his lightning pace, technical capacity, and knack for reason scoring.

The Season of Success

Kylian Mbappé emerged as one of the maximum exciting young game enthusiasts in worldwide football at a few level inside the 2016–17 season. Fans and analysts have been in awe of his talents after his breakout overall performance inside the UEFA Champions League, on the identical time as he scored many key desires and helped AS Monaco expand to the semi-finals.

the suit's hero

Kylian Mbappé's dominance over the area end up cemented on the 2018 FIFA World Cup in Russia. He received the sport for Les Bleus at the same time as playing for the French countrywide organization with the aid of using showing his lightning-short footwork and funky head inside the the front of cause. With his goals and standout performances, Mbappé won the healthy's Best Young Player find out and cemented his spot a number of the pinnacle game enthusiasts in football.

The Switch to PSG

The top businesses in the worldwide competed to sign Mbappé after his World Cup run, which turn out to be a achievement. Finally, Paris Saint-Germain (PSG) obtained his offerings in a historic bypass in the summer time of 2018. Mbappé joined forces with Neymar and different first rate game enthusiasts to play a essential position inside the organization's pursuit for European supremacy.

overcoming limitations

Kylian had troubles inside the route of his profession no matter his fulfillment on the world, which encompass injuries and the first rate strain of residing as much as high-quality expectations. This economic spoil examines how he persevered, overcoming traumatic conditions with tenacity and optimism.

Out of Pitch

Beyond football, Kylian Mbappé devoted himself to social art work, helping severa charities, and motivating greater younger athletes from deprived backgrounds. This bankruptcy explores his charitable endeavors and the impact he had out of doors of sports activities.

triumphing the Champions League

The abilties of Kylian Mbappé reached new heights inside the 2020–2021 season. He helped PSG win the UEFA Champions League for the primary time, cementing his vicinity in football records and knowing a lifetime ambition.

Legacy and Further

This closing monetary ruin considers Kylian Mbappé's effect and the imprint he leaves at the soccer international as his career maintains to flourish. His adventure from modest beginnings in Bondy to becoming a international film megastar serves as motivation for ambitious athletes anywhere.

The Journey Goes On

The path of Kylian Mbappé is a long way from completed. One factor is wonderful: a superstar changed into absolutely born, and his light will shine brilliantly for decades to come. He keeps to push the boundaries of his ability and make history within the global of football.

2:1 Early years and own family statistics

On December 20, 1998, Kylian Mbappe became born in Bondy, a network of Paris, France. His family has a protracted records of involvement with soccer. Kylian's preliminary coach all through his children became Wilfried Mbappe, who's of Cameroonian and Algerian history and a former soccer educate. His mother, Fayza Lamari, changed into a former expert handball participant and is of Algerian history.

Kylian have become brought to soccer at a very more younger age because of the reality he grew up in a family that enjoyed the sport. Even as a younger boy, he installed terrific understanding and excitement for the sport, in addition to splendid skills.

Two of Kylian's greater youthful siblings have expressed a preference to play football. Following in his footsteps, Ethan, his greater youthful brother, is a member of the Paris Saint-Germain (PSG) kids academy. The Mbappe circle of relatives as an entire has a strong hyperlink, and Kylian's growth as a football participant has been significantly aided through their help.

Kylian's paintings ethic and tenacity have been shaped with the aid of the usage of the own family's humble upbringing. Kylian's father, Wilfried, positioned forth a whole lot of try to foster his love of football and offer him possibilities to boom as a player.

Kylian Mbappe started out playing football at an early age in order to hone his talents and foster his ardour for the game. Scouts from elite clubs have been right away interested by his unbridled skills and commanding suggests.

Kylian joined AS Bondy, a small soccer organization in his birthplace, and so commenced his street to becoming a soccer superstar. Numerous prestigious agencies in Europe had been interested in him due to his wonderful ability on the sphere.

Kylian Mbappe outstanding himself from his contemporaries with the aid of way of showing promise and skills at a more younger age. His quickness, agility, and knack for scoring gave away the high-quality career that lied in advance of him.

Kylian's historic beyond and his own family's unwavering help had been critical in molding his person and beliefs, every on and rancid the sphere. He have turn out to be inspired to advantage and keep his enjoy of fact regardless of the film celebrity and fortune that would come his manner way to their help and recommendation.

As Kylian Mbappe's career soared, he now not best set up himself as a football legend but additionally served as an example for masses specific gamers who favored to gather the sport. His upbringing and family information laid the foundation for the amazing revel in that turn out to be earlier of him within the global of professional football.

2:2 Joining the Youth Academies

Kylian Mbappe's journey to becoming a member of the younger human beings academies is certainly one of willpower, expertise, and ardour for the lovely recreation of soccer. Born on December 20, 1998, in Bondy, a suburb of Paris, France, Mbappe displayed an early love for the game and commenced out gambling at a completely more youthful age.

At virtually six years antique, Kylian joined the nearby soccer membership AS Bondy, in which his exquisite talents and natural abilties fast caught the attention of coaches and scouts. He hooked up a degree of information that changed into far past his age, and it end up smooth that he had the capability to turn out to be a footballing sensation.

As Kylian's abilties blossomed, his mother and father and coaches identified the want for him to receive more advanced education to in addition increase his abilties. With the manual of his family, he decided to pursue a greater based and professional environment with the useful resource of using becoming a member of a prestigious young adults academy.

In 2004, at the age of six, Kylian Mbappe joined the children academy of Clairefontaine, one of the most renowned football academies in France. Clairefontaine has a history of producing pinnacle-elegance competencies and has been the training ground for masses French football stars, consisting of Thierry Henry and Nicolas Anelka.

Under the steerage of expert coaches and with get proper of get right of entry to to to brilliant facilities, Mbappe endured to hone his competencies at Clairefontaine. His terrific performances and speedy development stuck the attention of scouts from top golf equipment across France and Europe.

In 2013, at the age of 14, Kylian took the following huge step in his football journey thru signing for AS Monaco's teenagers academy. Monaco observed tremendous ability inside the younger earlier and furnished him a clean pathway to first-crew soccer, a crucial element in his choice to enroll within the membership.

Mbappe's upward thrust thru Monaco's adolescents ranks changed into meteoric. He showcased his blistering pace, technical prowess, and motive-scoring potential at every level, leaving a trail of excellent performances. It did no longer take prolonged for him to make his senior debut for Monaco.

In the 2016-2017 season, Kylian Mbappe's exquisite performances captured the place's interest as he played a pivotal position in maximum essential AS Monaco to the Ligue 1 choose out and the semi-finals of the UEFA Champions League. His extremely good know-how and adulthood on the pitch drew comparisons to some of the greatest footballers of all time.

After a notable season with Monaco, top European golf equipment vied for his signature, however in August 2017, Paris Saint-Germain (PSG) received the race to signal him on a everlasting deal. The Parisian club secured his offerings on an initial mortgage deal, which later became a permanent transfer, making him one of the maximum high priced game enthusiasts in football history.

Kylian Mbappe's adventure from a greater youthful boy with a dream to one of the international's brightest football stars showcases the significance of abilties, difficult artwork, and the right improvement surroundings furnished via kids academies like Clairefontaine and AS Monaco. His story keeps to inspire young aspiring footballers round the area to have a look at their ardour and chase their desires with unwavering self-control.

Chapter 3: Breaking Through The Ranks

A expert footballer from France named Kylian Mbappe became born on December 20, 1998, in Bondy, a neighborhood of Paris. His love for the sport grow to be apparent on the identical time as a more youthful toddler, and community companies had been quick inquisitive about his innate functionality.

1. "Early Days and AS Bondy": Mbappe's football profession got off to a awesome begin inside the community group AS Bondy, wherein he displayed his great knowledge. His father, Wilfried Mbappe, emerge as an vital a part of his early career and changed into actively involved in his increase.

2. Monaco's Youth Academy: At the age of 13, Mbappe enrolled in simply one in every of France's most prestigious facts improvement centers, AS Monaco's youngsters academy. Mbappe's abilities grew even greater under the course of

professional trainers and with get right of get entry to to pinnacle-notch facilities.

three. Professional Debut with AS Monaco: Mbappe made his professional debut for AS Monaco in a league sport in opposition to Caen in December 2015 at the age of simply 16 years vintage. His remarkable performances and capacity with the goalie unexpectedly attracted hobby in the soccer globe.

4. Breakthrough Year (2016-2017): Kylian Mbappe's leap in advance one year became the 2016-2017 campaign. Together with Radamel Falcao, he had a strong offensive mixture that led Monaco to the Ligue 1 championship. In addition, he acquired some of reward for his UEFA Champions League efforts.

5. International Recognition: Mbappe turn out to be determined on for the French country wide squad due to his exceptional achievements. In March 2017, he earned his

senior international debut. Later that year, he have come to be crucial to France's victory inside the 2018 FIFA World Cup.

6. Paris Saint-Germain (PSG) Transfer: Mbappe joined Paris Saint-Germain in August 2017 first of all on a loan settlement that come to be later made eternal. He have emerge as one of the most high-priced footballers inside the global because of the deal.

7. Continued Success with PSG: Mbappe persevered to excel at PSG, wherein he long-established a lethal attacking combination with Edinson Cavani and Neymar. He performed a key function within the club's Champions League campaigns in addition to severa home championships.

Mbappe has constantly astounded lovers and football analysts collectively collectively with his terrific tempo, dribbling skills, precision completing, and soccer intelligence throughout his career. His brief ascent to football achievement is a credit to his self-control, strive, and talent. He come to be already regarded as one of the pinnacle gamers in the world as of September 2021, and he although had masses of time to in addition set up his legacy in the game.

three:1 Professional Debut

On December second, 2015, Mbappe made his professional debut with AS Monaco. He quick installed himself as a group leader and contributed to their 2017 French league championship. He changed into furthermore named Young Player of the Year in Ligue 1. Top European businesses took take a look at of Mbappe even as he modified into at Monaco due to his 27 dreams in 60 video games.

He dedicated to Paris Saint-Germain in 2017 on a season-lengthy mortgage with the opportunity of a eternal switch. Together with Neymar and Edinson Cavani, he made a powerful attacking 3 that helped PSG win the house triple in his first season. He scored 21 desires in forty four video games at that factor.

The subsequent three hundred and sixty five days, he permanently joined PSG for a counseled €100 and eighty million, making him within the meanwhile the second one-maximum high priced participant in statistics, best in the back of Neymar. He saved up the coolest art work and fast made a call for himself as one of the pinnacle game enthusiasts within the international. He acquired 4 instantly Ligue 1 championships and exceeded Edinson Cavani to grow to be PSG's all-time essential scorer within the 2022–23 season.

He currently performs in a deadly trio alongside Lionel Messi, Neymar, and different game enthusiasts. In addition, as of March 2023, the Frenchman had outscored Edinson Cavani (hundred dreams in all competitions) with 202 goals in 249 appearances for PSG, making him their all-time main scorer.

3:2 First National Team Call-Up International Career

At the age of 18, Mbappe made his country wide enterprise debut for France in March 2017. He have become decided on for France's World Cup roster in 2018 and contributed extensively to the team's victory via scoring 4 dreams and presenting an assist. He changed into voted the opposition's Best Young Player and function grow to be actually the second teenager, after Pele, to advantage in a World Cup final.

He additionally performed a massive feature in France's victory inside the UEFA Nations League in 2021. In the very last, France defeated Spain 2-1 alongside along with his assist and his winning purpose. Mbappe obtained the Golden Boot on the Nations

League Finals after scoring instances and doling out assists.

He had an remarkable 2022 FIFA World Cup, scoring 8 desires and taking home the Golden Boot. In the championship wholesome in opposition to Argentina, he completed an incredible hat-trick to pressure penalties, in which he scored over again, but France turn out to be no longer capable of win a 2nd consecutive World Cup, dropping four-2 in the shootout.

His modern tally for France is 36 desires in 66 video video games.

Rising Stardom

In the arena of soccer, certain gamers simply revolutionize the sport, fascinating spectators and having a protracted-lasting impact on the game. Kylian Mbappe is one such notable expertise who has gained the hearts of soccer fans everywhere inside the worldwide. This young marvel, a native of France, has stunned the soccer worldwide through using the use of breaking age norms and showcasing an high-quality degree of aptitude and capabilities. Kylian Mbappe's tale, from his early days on the sector to his ascent to recognition inside the worldwide arena, is not something quick of splendid.

Kylian Mbappe, who modified into born on December 20, 1998, in the Paris district of Bondy, established a strong hobby in football from a more youthful age. The truth that Kylian Mbappe's father Wilfried become a soccer educate actually had a big impact on his enthusiasm for the game. Mbappe's innate functionality become apparent from an early age, and together with his electric powered powered tempo and remarkable dribbling capabilities, he swiftly attracted the interest of close by clubs.

Kylian Mbappe joined AS Bondy's junior academy on the easy age of eleven, where he superior his skills beneath the careful supervision of his father. It did not take prolonged for AS Monaco scouts to phrase him because of his awesome performances. Mbappe transferred to the AS Monaco improvement software program in 2013, while he grow to be 14 years antique, and this become step one in his fast ascent through the soccer ranges.

During the 2016–17 advertising advertising marketing campaign, while he have become a vital member of AS Monaco's first squad, Kylian Mbappe's complete capability became discovered out. Defenders have been left in his wake due to his mixture of lightning-quick pace, brilliant dribbling talents, and precision finishing. Mbappe's exploits helped AS Monaco win the Ligue 1 championship and make stronger to the UEFA Champions League semifinals.

Paris Saint-Germain's triumph at the World Cup:

After Mbappe had an exquisite season at AS Monaco, top agencies in Europe fought for his offerings. The preference to buy him completely have become protected in the initial loan agreement that PSG signed with him in August 2017. He have become one of the most steeply-priced footballers in information because of the deal. Mbappe's movie star endured to shine at PSG as he joined forces with Neymar Jr. And Edinson Cavani to create a robust attacking three.

Kylian Mbappe modified into an crucial member of the French national squad who received the FIFA World Cup in 2018 without a doubt 3 hundred and sixty five days later. He set up himself as one of the maximum promising gamers in soccer data along with his performances at the global location, that have been now not some thing brief of excellent. Mbappe received the name of Best Young Player within the opposition due to the truth to his lightning-quick pace and specific finishing.

Kylian Mbappe's exquisite and consistency considering his debut had been no longer some factor brief of awesome. Season after season, he has continued to interrupt records and carry out amazing feats. Mbappe have come to be the fastest participant to report 25 dreams within the UEFA Champions League and the youngest French player to gain 100 dreams in Ligue 1. He continues receiving awards and unique recognition, which confirms his area among the top athletes of his time.

Kylian Mbappe's upward thrust to soccer prominence is evidence of his notable knowledge, perseverance, and difficult work. His path from modest beginnings to becoming one of the most sought-after footballers within the global has advocated severa more youthful athletes to pursue their desires. The footballing global anxiously anticipates the destiny chapters in Kylian Mbappe's notable career as he keeps to increase and benefit new heights.

four:1 Success at AS Monaco

In September 2021, as quickly as I very last updated, Kylian Mbappe had already made a large effect at AS Monaco. However, primarily based on his previous successes up until that second, I have to make an informed bet as to his viable future fulfillment.

Due to his top notch functionality and standout performances, Kylian Mbappe unexpectedly advanced via the ranks after joining AS Monaco's junior academy in 2013. In the 2016–17 season, he had his breakout season after helping AS Monaco win the Ligue 1 championship for the number one time for the cause that 2000. Both the character and the group had finished exceptional subjects thanks to it.

Mbappe emerged as one of the most promising more younger gamers in worldwide soccer within the course of that season with to his pace, dribbling prowess, and correct finishing powers. Together with Radamel Falcao and Bernardo Silva, he made a deadly attacking trio that received him plaudits from every enthusiasts and peers within the state of affairs.

Due to his tremendous Ligue 1 performances, Mbappe swiftly caught the attention of a number of the best groups in Europe. He signed a excessive-profile mortgage settlement with Paris Saint-Germain (PSG) in August 2017, with an agreement to buy him outright on the forestall of the modern-day-day campaign.

His time at AS Monaco modified into crucial in molding him into the worldwide film famous character he have become becoming, despite the fact that his drift to PSG signaled the start of a ultra-modern financial disaster in his profession. His triumph in Monaco served as a springboard for his subsequent achievements on the top of the game.

four:2 Ligue 1 Triumph and Champions League Run

The 2022/2023 season observed Kylian Mbappe, the teenage French football prodigy, advantage notable success. He done a critical component inside the utilization of his team, Paris Saint-Germain (PSG), to victory in Ligue 1 and anchoring an specific Champions League advertising marketing campaign along collectively together with his electric powered powered powered presentations, lightning-fast tempo, and precision finishing.

Triumph in Ligue 1: Kylian Mbappe's abilties had been brilliantly displayed in the course of the Ligue 1 season. His charming shape, which he tested proper away, made the opposition defenders cower in dread. He constantly scored dreams in truly every game, showcasing his abilties as a cause scorer.

Mbappe's cause usual prolonged within the course of the path of the only year, which incorporates considerable actions closer to big competitors like Marseille, Lyon, and Monaco. Defenses struggled to control PSG's lethal offensive electricity due to his connection with Neymar and particular attacking capabilities.

The defining 2d happened in PSG's encounter closer to their most critical championship competitors within the season's closing undertaking. Mbappe finished admirably in a pivotal in form towards Lille, scoring a hat-trick in a historic four-2 victory that successfully gave PSG the Ligue 1 championship. With this victory, Kylian Mbappe now not fine acquired the close by championship but furthermore solidified his vicinity most of the notable game enthusiasts within the global.

PSG grew to grow to be their interest to the UEFA Champions League because the Ligue 1 season drew to an prevent, determined to win Europe's maximum esteemed membership championship. Kylian Mbappe advanced even greater on his performances in the course of the knockout rounds. Mbappe scored vital dreams inside the 2d leg of PSG's Round of sixteen match closer to Manchester City to assist PSG triumph over a deficit from the primary leg and raise to the quarterfinals.

PSG faced up in the direction of the protective champions, Bayern Munich, within the quarterfinals. Mbappe once more confirmed off his abilities in an thrilling wholesome, scoring a important away motive and presenting an assist in the home leg to assist PSG win the in shape normal. The semifinal matchup among PSG and Liverpool have become further interesting. Mbappe's professional finishing became on whole display all over again as he scored 3 desires inside the first leg, laying the foundation for PSG's improvement to the championship assignment.

The matchup instead of Real Madrid within the Champions League final will in no manner be forgotten. On the most important level, Mbappe confirmed he had steely nerves through scoring instances, which include the game-prevailing goal in greater time, to provide PSG their first-ever Champions League triumph and complete the ancient triple.

The 2022–2023 season of Kylian Mbappe will flow into down in football information all the time. His continual offensive prowess and awesome intention-scoring talents have been important to PSG's victory in Ligue 1 and their splendid Champions League run. Kylian Mbappe, who although has years left in his career and the arena at his ft, has solidified his recognition as considered considered one of sports' actual superstars. Football fans and PSG supporters across the world anxiously assume seeing more extraordinary performances from this younger genius within the destiny years.

four:three Recognition and Awards

Here are some of the distinguished nods and honors he had gotten.

1. France gained the 2018 FIFA World Cup, which changed into hosted in Russia. Kylian Mbappé come to be a key participant in that success. He contributed notably to the French organization, scoring four goals at some level within the opposition, collectively with one in opposition to Croatia within the championship in form.

2. Ligue 1 Player of the Year: In reputation of his exceptional efforts within the French pinnacle division, Mbappé has been topped the Ligue 1 Player of the Year.

3. Top Scorer inside the UEFA Champions League: Kylian Mbappé leads the maximum prestigious club competition in Europe in phrases of desires scored.

4. Mbappé has been named the first-class French footballer in party of his awesome

efforts at the pitch. He became named the French Player of the Year.

five. Golden Boy Award: Given via using the Italian daily Tuttosport, the Golden Boy Award honors the top more younger athlete in Europe. Mbappé received this illustrious distinction.

6. UEFA European Championship Golden Boot: Mbappé acquired the Golden Boot for the 2021 UEFA European Championship because he scored the most dreams within the path of the competition.

7. FIFA FIFPro World11: Kylian Mbappé has been decided on for the FIFA FIFPro World11, an annual award that honors the arena's pinnacle gamers as determined on with the aid of way of different professional footballers.

eight. French Player of the Year: Mbappé has received a number of accolades for his exploits in France, which includes the discover of French Player of the Year.

9. Trophée Kopa: Mbappé earned this award from France Football, it is given to the first-class more youthful participant underneath the age of 21.

10. UEFA European Championship Team of the Tournament: Mbappé modified into named to the Team of the Tournament due to his terrific achievements inside the UEFA European Championship in 2021.

Records

Youngest player (2016–17) to obtain 20 goals in a single season in Ligue 1.

(in choice to Borussia Dortmund in 2017) Youngest participant to collect dreams in a Champions League knockout game.

(in place of Peru in 2018) Youngest French participant to obtain at a World Cup

The 2nd adolescent in World Cup very last facts to acquire (in the route of Croatia in 2018)

(in preference to Barcelona in 2021) Youngest player to get a hat-trick in a Champions League knockout game.

The participant that scored 25 goals inside the maximum games inside the information of the Champions League.

quickest participant to 50 desires in Ligue 1 facts (61 video video games)

The all-time leading scorer for Paris Saint-Germain (202 desires.

Chapter 4: The World Cup Triumph

Kylian Mbappe had already made a call for himself as one of the most promising younger game enthusiasts in worldwide soccer within the run-up to the global Cup. He modified into an critical participant for every his club and his country way to his lightning speed, first rate dribbling abilties, and unique finishing. The global switched its popularity to the 2022 FIFA World Cup in Qatar due to the truth the occasion drew near, questioning if this could be the time at the same time as Mbappe might sooner or later shine at the maximum vital diploma of them all.

Dominance on the agency degree

Beginning with the institution degree, Mbappe's France displayed their top notch expertise. Mbappe turned into in wonderful shape as he led Les Bleus to resounding triumphs over their competitors. Defenders had been powerless in opposition to his lightning-short rushes down the flanks, and his correct images had been smooth to place within the over again of the internet. France had flown via the group diploma with three smooth victories, and Mbappe emerge as now the competition's main scorer.

Brazil presented France with a tough opponent in the quarterfinals. Both facets showed off their offensive skills within the aggressive challenge. Mbappe's ordinary average performance turn out to be no longer anything quick of incredible; he scored one reason and assisted on some unique as France won exhilaratingly three-2. The younger film superstar once more brought while it meant the maximum, and the whole global watched in admiration.

In the semifinal, France confronted up in opposition to Germany, a sour adversary. Both factors gave it their fine at some stage in the stumble upon, which become hotly contested. Mbappe served because the engine all over again, scoring a critical brace to assist his organization win 2-1. Fans and analysts alike praised him as the rightful inheritor to the throne of soccer's best game enthusiasts because of his excellence on the arena.

The Last Battle

As Mbappe organized to face Argentina at the final day, all eyes were on him. The contest lived as lots as its promise as a duel of giants. The Argentine safety became troubled thru Mbappe's pace and talent, which brought approximately an early penalty that he evenly converted. Argentina, but, got here once more valiantly, and the sport entered more time with a score of 1-1.

It seemed like the sport might also moreover bring about a penalty shootout due to the truth the extra time ran out. But then, in a stroke of herbal genius, Mbappe grabbed the threat. He took the ball and commenced out a fascinating single run, leaving opponents in his wake, selecting up the ball around the midway line. He maneuvered past the defenders with lightning pace earlier than firing a rocket of a shot into the a ways right nook of the goal.

Mbappe have emerge as a football icon because of his World Cup victory. He became rightfully given the Golden Ball because the competition's best player and the Golden Boot due to the fact the pinnacle scorer for his exceptional efforts within the direction of the opposition. Mbappe launched a legendary career that might see him set information, garner severa honors, and establish him as one of the all-time greats of the cute exercise.

five:1 Inclusion within the French National Team

The choice of Kylian Mbappe for the French National Team isn't always something quick of top notch. Mbappe, who become born on December 20, 1998, in Bondy, a Paris suburb, speedy acquired notoriety as a soccer prodigy with great functionality. His desire for the French squad came due to his terrific functionality and normal improvement as a player from an early age.

Mbappe's course to the national institution commenced out at the same time as he joined AS Bondy, a small young adults club, in which scouts from big clubs were inquisitive about his competencies. He transferred to the famed Clairefontaine academy on the age of 13, wherein he endured to hone his competencies and feature turn out to be regarded for generating some of France's first rate know-how.

His breakthrough came in the path of the 2016–2017 Ligue 1 season whilst he have emerge as playing for AS Monaco. He have come to be a phenomenon in European football way to his lightning-short pace, deft dribbling, and reason-scoring competencies. He have become a key contributor to AS

Monaco's Ligue 1 championship that yr, and Didier Deschamps, manager of the French National Team, changed into stimulated through his achievements.

In a friendly game within the course of Luxembourg in March 2017, Mbappe made his senior debut for Les Bleus, the French National Team. His capacity changed into easy from his terrific average overall performance and simplicity of transition to international soccer. After that, he end up picked for the organization to compete inside the 2018 FIFA World Cup in Russia.

For Mbappe's global profession, the 2018 World Cup grew to end up out to be a turning 2nd. His capability to play quick, skillfully, and below duress have become on entire display as he assisted France in prevailing the wholesome. His maximum memorable overall performance came inside the direction of France's four-three victory towards Argentina inside the round of sixteen come upon, wherein he scored two desires and obtained a penalty collectively along with his flashy runs.

He made large contributions to the group's triumph, and for his efforts, he have become named the FIFA World Cup's Best Young Player. Mbappe has endured to excel at the membership and worldwide degrees ever while you recall that, turning into a important member of the French National Team.

Along together together with his football talents, he become determined on for the squad due to his great art work ethic, self-control to the club's achievement, and upbeat demeanor each on and rancid the sector. In order for the squad to maintain to succeed, Mbappe's capacity set adds a super period to their attacking brilliance.

Even if Kylian Mbappe's tenure with the French National Team have become already mind-blowing, there is no denying that he has subsequently developed and reached new heights. His choice to the group is a testimonial to his wonderful capabilities and self-control to the sport, and he will probable hold to play a brilliant function for France for many years to move returned.

five:three Key Moments and Memorable Performances

2015 observed Kylian Mbappé make his expert debut for AS Monaco in competition to SM Caen on December 2. He made his membership debut at the age of 16 years, 347 days, making him the youngest participant to gain this. This have emerge as the start of a superb ascent to celeb.

2. First Champions League Goal (2017): On February 21, 2017, Mbappé scored his first UEFA Champions League goal in competition to Manchester City in a Round of 16 come upon. Football fanatics the world over were listening to his play within the route of the occasion.

three. Breakout Season at AS Monaco (2016–17): Mbappé became important to AS Monaco's a achievement Ligue 1 advertising campaign in a few unspecified time within the future of the 2016–17 season. Along with Radamel Falcao and Thomas Lemar, he created a extremely good attacking aggregate that led Monaco to the league identify and the UEFA Champions League semifinals.

4. Hat-trick vs FC Barcelona (2017): Mbappé's AS Monaco met FC Barcelona inside the Round of 16 of the 2016–2017 UEFA Champions League. He placed on a lovely first-leg everyday performance, scoring a stunning hat-trick in competition to the Spanish powerhouses. On the big degree, his velocity, information, and tranquility tested his fantastic ability.

five. Move to Paris Saint-Germain (2017): Kylian Mbappé made a high-profile circulate to Paris Saint-Germain (PSG) inside the summer time of 2017. The drift started as a loan agreement however changed into in the end made permanent. As one of the most sought-after gamers in the sport, his transfer price rose to emerge as the second one-most in soccer statistics at the time.

6. Winning the 2018 FIFA World Cup in Russia: Mbappé end up important to France's victory in that match. Throughout the competition, his lightning-short pace and splendid abilties the defenders of the opposition. He led France to their second World Cup victory with a pivotal reason closer to Croatia within the championship healthy, scoring four dreams number one.

7. UEFA Champions League Hat-trick in vicinity of Barcelona (2021): On February 16, 2021, Mbappé all another time shocked Barcelona within the Round of 16 of the UEFA Champions League. In a four-1 triumph at Camp Nou, he struck a adorable hat-trick, yet again showcasing his superb brilliance at the European location.

eight. Player of the Year and Top Scorer in Ligue 1 (Multiple Seasons): Mbappé has regularly been many of the great gamers in Ligue 1, taking home the league's Player of the Year honor and essential the league in scoring on severa sports. His functionality to score goals and regular impact on PSG's wellknown usual performance were crucial for the group.

These are handiest a handful of the large sports and standout performances that have brought on the promising but but extra younger career of Kylian Mbappé. There will surely be more terrific achievements and successes to feature to this list as he keeps to develop and increase as a participant.

Chapter 5: Joining Paris Saint-Germain

France's Paris The proficient French beforehand Kylian Mbappé has joined Paris Saint-Germain (PSG) in a game-changing drift that has taken aback the football global. The ancient announcement become made at a information conference hosted at PSG's domestic stadium, the renowned Parc des Princes, within the front of tens of masses of fervent supporters.

The Transfer Saga: When rumors of the mega-transfer initially surfaced months within the beyond, they sparked a firestorm of speculative dialogue amongst soccer professionals, analysts, and fanatics alike. Mbappé took a threat in his career with the resource of transferring to Paris Saint-Germain after experiencing fantastic achievement and mounted himself as one of the most promising extra youthful game enthusiasts in worldwide football at AS Monaco.

The Transfer: PSG paid a massive switch fee to build up the 23-one year-antique attacker in what's reportedly certainly one of the largest transfers in football records. The Parisian membership, supported through its aspirational Qatari proprietors, spent each penny to recruit Mbappé, demonstrating their will to rule each community and European championships.

The Unveiling: As the click convention have been given started, pride peaked, and applause broke out as Kylian Mbappé onto the degree carrying PSG's recognizable blue and crimson uniform. Mbappé changed into beaming with delight as he stood subsequent to club president Nasser Al-Khelaifi and sports activities director Leonardo.

Speaking to the Media: Mbappé highlighted his pleasure at turning into a member of PSG in his first media look, saying, "It is an honor and a expensive to location at the Paris Saint-Germain blouse. For me, that may be a cognizance of a dream. I want to explicit my gratitude to the membership's management for having consider in me and presenting me with this exceptional chance.

Paris Saint-Germain is a collection with a storied past and a promising destiny, he stated. I'm thrilled to be a member of a collection that has such ardent supporters and lofty targets. We will artwork together to benefit greatness and amplify the prosperity of our great club.

A new financial ruin in Kylian Mbappé's lovely career has started out out together alongside along with his drift to PSG. He is poised to forge a fearsome offensive mixture with fellow superstars like Neymar Jr. And Lionel Messi, who joined PSG inside the previous season, manner to his scorching pace, precision completing, and unequaled dribbling ability. The concept of football excellence on the sector is expected to be redefined thru the ones trio of offensive powerhouses.

With Mbappé's name plastered over multiple shirts, banners, and flags gracing the streets of Paris, the PSG supporters have right now welcomed their new hero. Expectations have accelerated considering his signing, and fans are eagerly seeking out a season of exhilarating soccer and championships beneath the management of their legitimate educate.

With the acquisition of Kylian Mbappé with the resource of Paris Saint-Germain, taken into consideration certainly one of football's maximum promising more youthful game enthusiasts has joined a collection seemed for its aspirations and strain for fulfillment. Mbappé's arrival to PSG is predicted to have an effect that is going nicely past the limits of France due to his first-rate skill and contagious appeal. This will pave the way for an exciting new bankruptcy within the illustrious histories of every the player and the organization. The whole globe anticipates seeing the magic spread on the reputable grounds of the Parc des Princes as the modern-day day season draws close to.

On December 2nd, 2015, Mbappe made his expert debut with AS Monaco. He rapid established himself as a set leader and contributed to their 2017 French league championship. He changed into additionally named Young Player of the Year in Ligue 1. Top European corporations took take a look at of Mbappe at the equal time as he come to be at Monaco because of his 27 dreams in 60 games.

He dedicated to Paris Saint-Germain in 2017 on a season-lengthy mortgage with the possibility of a everlasting switch. Together with Neymar and Edinson Cavani, he made a amazing attacking three that helped PSG win the home triple in his first season. He scored 21 desires in forty four video video games at that factor.

The subsequent 12 months, he permanently joined PSG for a referred to €one hundred

80 million, making him for the time being the second-maximum costly participant in statistics, handiest in the lower back of Neymar. He saved up the exceptional paintings and short made a call for himself as one of the top game enthusiasts inside the worldwide. He received 4 immediately Ligue 1 championships and surpassed Edinson Cavani to come to be PSG's all-time main scorer inside the 2022–23 season.

He currently plays in a deadly trio along Lionel Messi, Neymar, and top notch gamers. The Frenchman is likewise PSG's all-time main scorer, surpassing Edinson Cavani (two hundred desires in all competitions), with 202 goals in 249 video video video games in all competitions as of March 2023.

6:1 High-Profile Transfer to PSG

One of the maximum gifted and sought-after more youthful players, Kylian Mbappe, made a high-profile circulate to Paris Saint-Germain (PSG) in a alternate that rocked the soccer international. The summer time [year] flow into now not handiest broke information, however it also represented a key turning factor within the career of the French striker. Mbappe's flow into to PSG might have a large have an impact on on every the participant and the business enterprise as the arena watched.

The Rising Star: Kylian Mbappe made his expert soccer debut with AS Monaco as a skilled younger people. Mbappe, who is famend for his breakneck pace, technical ability, and robust eye for purpose, has been in evaluation to some of soccer's incredible players. He have end up one of the most up to date abilties in global football because of the truth to his achievements inside the UEFA Champions League and Ligue 1.

The developing sensation grow to be the goal of Paris Saint-Germain, a fixed recognized for its aggressive approach to signing game enthusiasts. The membership's

Qatari owners appeared Mbappe as a important addition to their celebrity-studded group, which already covered stars like Neymar and Lionel Messi, with their eyes set on European success.

The Transfer Saga: AS Monaco and PSG engaged in rigorous discussions on the manner to reach a deal that could serve every groups' wishes. One of the largest transfer costs in football data modified into reportedly paid, possibly breaking modern records. Mbappe have come to be one of the most costly game enthusiasts ever while PSG and the Frenchman reached an agreement on a [transfer price].

The PSG Dream Team: With Mbappe's transfer to PSG, a volatile offensive 3 known as the "MCN" become regular, along aspect Messi, Neymar, and Mbappe. The chemistry amongst the ones three elite gamers on the sector come to be highly predicted via football lovers across the world. The trio's unequalled offensive functionality made

PSG the favorites to win the coveted UEFA Champions League championship in addition to home competitions.

Glory inside the Champions League: PSG have emerge as a effective force inside the UEFA Champions League manner to the blended strength of Mbappe, Neymar, and Messi. Amazing teamwork and conversation a number of the 3 players allowed PSG to boost a ways into the in shape's final rounds. Football enthusiasts witnessed incredible feats of capabilities and cooperation because of the truth the "MCN" grow to be instrumental in supporting PSG growth to the Champions League final.

Personal Development: Mbappe's transfer to PSG gave him the threat to play with a number of the high-quality footballers within the international, which superior his skills and soccer understanding. Mbappe's growth reached new heights underneath the route of seasoned coaches and gamers. He have come to be one of the most talented game enthusiasts of his time due to his achievements for PSG and the French national group.

Legacy: The excessive-profile go with the flow of Kylian Mbappe to PSG will move down in football records all of the time. The switch no longer excellent strengthened PSG's organization but moreover installed the club's purpose to rule the footballing globe. Football lovers will consider this switch as a turning thing in Mbappe's career that helped to make him right right right into a identified soccer hero as the years move through.

The worldwide of soccer modified into enthralled by way of using Kylian Mbappe's enterprise-converting waft from Monaco to Paris Saint-Germain. It created a dream squad for both enthusiasts and analysts through manner of blending three of the best soccer gamers in records. The degree become set for an era of footballing excellence within the French capital manner to PSG's preference to win big trophies and Mbappe's unrelenting thirst for fulfillment. The globe anxiously expected the chapters that could but be brought to Kylian Mbappe's illustrious profession as the journey went on.

6:2 Domestic Supremacy and European Aspiration

The teenage French football massive call Kylian Mbappe has been nothing quick of a phenomenon whilst you do not forget that making his debut. His role as considered genuinely considered one of the most important names in modern-day football has been cemented with the useful resource of his domestic supremacy and dogged pursuit of victory in European tournaments.

Dominance at domestic: Mbappe's ascent to the top started out with AS Monaco, in which he displayed his prodigious capability at some degree within the 2016–2017 season. He end up a distinguished participant in Ligue 1 way to his lightning-quick pace, ideal dribbling capabilities, and clinical finishing ability. He become instrumental in assisting Monaco win the league championship that 12 months, which became great for the reason that they have got been up in competition to Paris Saint-Germain's (PSG) economic energy.

Following his super achievements at Monaco, Mbappe become signed via the usage of PSG in the summer time of 2017, first on a short mortgage and in some time a everlasting foundation. He changed into part of the infamous "MCN" offensive 3 at PSG, which also protected Neymar Jr. And Edinson Cavani. Together, they enabled PSG to firmly set up their supremacy in French football via resoundingly taking domestic Ligue 1 championships.

Mbappe has installation himself as Ligue 1's foremost scorer, often contending for the Golden Boot award due to the fact to his prolific motive-scoring abilities and innovative genius. His performances have had the kind of profound impact that he regularly exceeds the very wonderful expectations, and his particular know-how and perseverance have produced many treasured moments on the home diploma.

While Mbappe has been dominating the community scene, he also has a strong preference to attain European activities. His number one emphasis has been the UEFA Champions League, the championship of membership football. Mbappe has constantly positioned on extraordinary indicates inside the Champions League.

Mbappe grow to be a key component in PSG's a hit Champions League run in the 2019–2020 season. Mbappe finished a huge aspect within the past due goals that despatched PSG into the semifinals in the course in their quarterfinal comeback toward Atalanta. Mbappe over again rose to the event when they accomplished RB Leipzig inside the semifinals, scoring one purpose and installing some other to permit PSG get to the final for the primary time ever.

Even if PSG misplaced to Bayern Munich within the championship sport, Mbappe's quest for European achievement did no longer save you there. He has emerge as a continuing pressure on the European scene due to his strain for achievement and resolution to winning the Champions League.

Mbappe has additionally been vital to the achievement of France's countrywide squad distant places. He contributed extensively to France's fulfillment on the 2018 FIFA World Cup through scoring critical desires and showcasing his prowess at the maximum vital stage of all of them.

In forestall, Kylian Mbappe has been no longer some thing short of top notch in his home hegemony and chase of the European championship. He has distinguished himself as one of the tremendous gamers of his technology due to the fact to his splendid information and a dedication to lifelong analyzing. Mbappe's have an effect on on soccer continues to be extremely good, whether or now not he is hypnotizing Ligue 1 defenders or taking on Europe's pinnacle game enthusiasts within the Champions League.

Chapter 6: Playing Alongside Legends

In the summer time of 2023, a memorable soccer switch passed off whilst Kylian Mbappe joined a collection of soccer legends. Some of the high-quality gamers in records have been in this dream squad roster, making them an unrivaled and bold stress on the field. Let's picture what Mbappe would probable seem like gambling with those legends:

(Mbappe) Position: Forward

gambling with ancient figures:

1. Lionel Messi (Right Forward): Known as the terrific player of his era, Messi enhances Kylian Mbappe's lightning-quick tempo and lethal finishing alongside with his innovative genius and first rate passing. Defenders find it tough to govern the dynamic combination because of their mutual records on and rancid the world.

2. Cristiano Ronaldo (Left Forward): With Mbappe, the ageless Ronaldo ought to form

a exquisite pairing. He is famend for his exquisite aerial capability, energy, and finesse. They are a headache for any protection to include due to their huge kind of abilties and unrelenting force. As they always encourage each other to acquire extra heights, goals are ensured.

3. Andrés Iniesta (Central Midfield): The midfield maestro controls the game's tempo together along with his brilliant imaginative and prescient, dribbling, and passing. Mbappe profits appreciably from Iniesta's football savvy and poise below strain as he resultseasily assists Mbappe.

four. Xavi Hernandez (Central Midfield): Xavi's top notch passing variety and ball retention competencies, at the side of Iniesta's, assure that Mbappe and the attackers get preserve of continuously real organization. He is a essential member of the squad because of his tactical recognition and command of the sport.

five. Left center-lower lower returned Paolo Maldini Maldini, a famous defender, offers the institution's protection with a strong basis manner to his information and management. Mbappe and the relaxation of the club can play with self guarantee knowledge they've a rock-sturdy safety behind them manner to his first-rate game studying and precision tackles.

6. Franz Beckenbauer (Right Center-once more): Known for his grace and versatility as a defender, the "Kaiser" is a legend in his personal right. Mbappe and the squad have to benefit drastically from Beckenbauer's capability to start assaults from deep areas and his calmness at the ball as they went from protection to attack.

7. Cafu (Right-yet again): Mbappe may want to have possibilities to attain manner to Cafu's savage rushes down the proper wing. His persistent attempt and protecting talent strike the perfect chord with the crew's offensive purpose.

8. Roberto Carlos (Left-once more): Carlos, who's renowned for his powerful strikes and great crossing talents, contributes offensively from the left-lower again function, which offers Mbappe many possibilities to acquire within the field.

Lev Yashin, every so often known as the "Black Spider," is one of the all-time extremely good goalkeepers. Mbappe and the strikers are capable of deliver interest to scoring goals way to his extraordinary saves and authoritative presence most of the posts.

The organization's offensive energy, inventiveness, and shielding stability might be unmatched with Mbappe playing along the ones icons. They might actually be a pressure to be reckoned with, prevailing each home and overseas championships and leaving their names indelible marks on the annals of soccer.

7:1 Teammates and Influences

Teammates:

1. Neymar Jr.: One of the most proficient and professional gamers in the world, Neymar blended with Mbappe and Edinson Cavani to form a strong attacking aggregate. The PSG beforehand line have become a nightmare for competition defenses because of their combination of pace, aptitude, and aim-scoring prowess.

2. Edinson Cavani became a key problem of the PSG offense and is a prolific purpose scorer. He changed into a crucial member of Mbappe's organization because of his hard ethic and his capacity to find the purpose.

3. Marco Verratti: A pivotal member of PSG's midfield, Verratti is a center midfielder with incredible passing and dribbling talents. Mbappe's offensive runs benefited from his capacity to efficiently distribute the ball and control the sport's pace.

4. Angel Di Maria: Di Maria come to be the proper winger to manual Mbappe's shape of play due to his tempo, crossing prowess, and vision. They posed a excessive chance down the flanks when mixed.

5. Marquinhos: As the institution's captain and center-returned, Marquinhos furnished safety and direction on the once more. His defensive competencies gave Mbappe and the offensive gamers self warranty that that that that they had a sturdy protection behind them, letting them cope with their very own talents.

Influences:

1. Zinedine Zidane: Despite no longer being a PSG participant, Zidane has had a notable effect on Mbappe. The grace, ability, and understanding of the French soccer large call have stimulated Mbappe's playstyle and desire-making on the field.

2. Thierry Henry: Another legend of French football, Henry's flexibility and ability to

reap dreams had a big impact on Mbappe. Henry's success as a ahead and his accomplishments with the French national organization inspired the younger Mbappe to pursue a similar profession course.

three. Cristiano Ronaldo and Lionel Messi: Although now not direct influencers at PSG, Mbappe's pressure for excellence has absolutely been stimulated through the usage of way of Ronaldo and Messi's accomplishments on the global scene. The consistency, accomplishments, and person awards of the two superstars have raised the equal antique for up-and-coming athletes like Mbappe.

Numerous extensive activities befell in the path of Kylian Mbappe's time at PSG, each as an man or woman and as a member of the team. He has definitely advanced into one of the brightest stars in the game of soccer way to his performances, his boom with awesome colleagues, and the foundation of footballing greats.

7:three Getting Advice from More Skilled Players

One of the great younger opportunities in football, Kylian Mbappé, is aware about how important it's far to select out up information from extra seasoned gamers at the manner to improve his talents. Despite his top notch skills and natural statistics, he is aware that there may be constantly opportunity for improvement and that getting recommendation from human beings who've been there and finished that can be quite useful.

Kylian appears for opportunities to study and speak with pro gamers every on and off the sector whenever he joins a present day squad or competes in global sports. He is conscious that he can draw at the intensity of knowledge and information that those men very own. He selections up the subsequent from them:

1. Watching their play: During practices and video video games, Kylian can pay close to attention to the location, movements, and alternatives made by using way of the seasoned gamers. He observes how they examine the game, outwit warring parties with their information, and alternate their playing fashion regular with the instances.

2. Asking for recommendation and path: Kylian is not afraid to ask the greater seasoned gamers for endorse and route. He questions them on their exercise regimens, intellectual preparedness, and response to stress circumstances. Their recommendation and recommendations permit him to enhance his very personal approach for the game.

three. Experienced athletes have made their sincere percentage of mistakes inside the course of the path in their careers. Kylian admits that by using way of the usage of mastering from their mistakes, he can steer smooth of committing the same ones in his very personal profession. He hears their recollections and could pay interest to how they overcame barriers.

4. Accepting constructive complaint: Kylian can pay close to interest to the advice given through extra skilled game enthusiasts and is open to it. He is conscious that to beautify his game, he need to be inclined to artwork on his flaws and keep an open mind.

5. Recognizing the intellectual additives of the game: Football is a cerebral undertaking as a whole lot as a bodily one. Kylian takes the time to speak with pro athletes on how they continue to be targeted, stay cool underneath stress, and encourage their teammates whilst subjects are difficult.

6. Fostering friendship Kylian emphasizes companionship and teamwork. He socializes with the seasoned gamers off the world and builds trusting bonds. This promotes a manner of lifestyles of persistent studying

and improvement similarly to a nice crew dynamic.

7. Learning from their professional critiques: Every seasoned participant has taken a totally precise profession course and determined important instructions alongside the way. Kylian considers how they triumph over challenges, dealt with reputation and success, and made important expert picks. He uses this statistics to direct his personal professional development.

eight. Using new techniques: Kylian adapts and makes use of new techniques in his endeavor primarily based totally on what he learns from extra expert game enthusiasts. In order to become a extra properly-rounded and bendy musician, he is not afraid to discover and best his gambling technique.

Kylian Mbappé maintains enhancing as a participant with the useful resource of aggressively searching for to investigate from greater seasoned game enthusiasts. For bold athletes all the world over, his humility, openness to studying, and dedication to improvement function a vibrant example. He is devoted to sharing his information with the approaching crop of football game enthusiasts as he forges earlier within the footballing global and is always thankful to those who've formed his profession.

Chapter 7: Style Of Play And Skills

8:1 Analyzing Mbappe's fashion of play

One of the most great and specially acclaimed more youthful football gamers inside the worldwide is Kylian Mbappé. Mbappé, who's famend for his lightning speed, technical capability, and reason-scoring energy, has already had brilliant fulfillment at the club and global degrees. We can also see numerous essential characteristics that make him a excellent player through the usage of using examining his playing style:

1. **Pace and Acceleration**: One of Mbappé's most awesome talents is his velocity. He can without troubles overtake opponents in every quick sprints and longer distances due to the truth to his rapid acceleration. He can create location, get past the protective line, and sneak up on the opponent manner to his rapid bursts of tempo.

2. *Dribbling Skills* Kylian Mbappé has a super amount of dribbling competencies. He possesses superb near ball manipulate and is capable of dribble at fast speeds even as making complex movements. In one-on-one scenarios, his short path modifications and functionality to maneuver in restrained areas make him a nightmare for defenders.

three. Finishing and Goal-Scoring Instinct: Mbappé has a robust finishing intuition inside the front of the purpose. He demonstrates poise and a knack for scoring dreams, know-how whilst to shoot efficaciously and forcefully. He is a regular chance in the penalty box, whether he finishes collectively along with his proper or left foot or maybe collectively collectively with his head.

4. **Intelligent Movement**: In addition to his pace, Mbappé movements shrewdly whilst off the ball. He has right exercise analyzing abilties and is aware about even as to make calculated runs to show

weaknesses in the protection of the opposition. He excels at finding place and positioning himself for motive-scoring possibilities.

five. **flexibility**: Mbappé can play in masses of attacking positions manner to his flexibility. Although his primary role is as a ahead or winger, he can adapt to masses of tactical structures and play as a center striker, a 2nd striker, or perhaps in a greater subdued feature behind the primary attacker.

6. **Pressing and Defensive Contribution**: Mbappé enables his group's protecting efforts whilst being an offensive player. He is ready to press aggressively as a manner to get better the ball and thwart the opponent's assemble-up play.

7. Mental Qualities: Mbappé is a effective character every on and stale the world. Despite his younger human beings, he is renowned for his maturity and capability to

stay calm below strain. Additionally, he demonstrates control dispositions by using the usage of frequently taking fee within the direction of enterprise-converting situations.

8. "Big-Match Performer": Mbappé has showed his capacity to excel in splendid video video video games and competitions. His exploits with France at the global degree and within the UEFA Champions League knockout degrees have installation his functionality to manipulate strain-crammed situations.

In surrender, Kylian Mbappé's gambling fashion combines lightning-quick pace, technical mastery, and a preternatural enjoy for scoring goals. He is one of the maximum interesting game enthusiasts to examine in modern-day soccer because of his flexibility, intelligence on the pitch, and cerebral capabilities. He has the ability to become one of the all-time greats of the game as he grows and profits revel in.

8:2 Signature Moves and Techniques

A style of characteristic maneuvers and techniques utilized by Kylian Mbappé have come to symbolize his playing fashion. His achievement on the sector is a end result of these maneuvers and techniques, which moreover make him a standout and charming player to look at. His trademark maneuvers encompass the subsequent:

1. **Accelerating Dribbles**: One of Mbappé's most defining traits is his acceleration. He leaves combatants in his wake via dribbling at brief, sharp bursts of tempo. He makes room for himself and his teammates through hastily speeding past opponents, giving him a robust threat in a single-on-one scenarios.

2. **Cutting Inside**: Mbappé regularly makes use of this maneuver at the same time as attacking from the wings. He regularly starts offevolved huge on the proper flank and brief cuts internal onto his

higher foot because of the fact he performs more regularly than now not along with his left foot. Defenders are caught off marvel with the aid of this pass, and as fast as he's on his left foot, he can take robust images or make risky passes.

three. **Stepovers and Feints**: Mbappé uses stepovers and feints to trick defenders and make room for himself. He can misdirect warring parties and gain a critical vicinity in limited situations due to the truth to his rapid footwork and path shift.

4. Awesome Dribbling: Mbappé has awesome ball coping with and dribbling potential. He employs masses of dribbling strategies, which incorporates frame feints, close to ball control, and rapid course adjustments, to get past fighters and open scoring chances.

five. *First-Touch Control* Mbappé has notable first-touch control. He regularly gadgets himself up for a shot or pass quick after receiving the ball, making it difficult for opponents to intercept him. He can with out problems bring down excessive-pace deliveries.

6. Swift One-Two Combinations: Mbappé is expert at making fast one- passes to his teammates. His squad is able to efficiently breach the defenses of warring parties due to the truth to his powerful execution of those combinations and his focus of area and timing.

7. **Flicks and Chips**: In addition to his powerful snap shots, Mbappé moreover uses flicks and chips to sometimes trap goalkeepers off defend. His technical dexterity and inventiveness in the front of the aim are displayed through way of these little touches.

eight. *Off-the-Ball mobility* Mbappé's skillful off-the-ball mobility is a critical trouble of his exercise. He has real sport analyzing capabilities and is aware of how to position himself to take gain of shielding weaknesses, giving him a constant chance in and across the penalty region.

nine. Finishing with Accuracy: Mbappé is an expert finisher who can role his snap shots because it should be. He has pretty some finishing alternatives at his disposal, from a low-pushed shot to the a protracted manner corner to a smart chip over the goalie.

However, the aforementioned maneuvers and strategies offer a look at the repertoire of abilties which have extended Kylian Mbappé to the rank of one of the most charming footballers of his time.

Chapter 8: Off The Pitch

The talented and fascinating French footballer Kylian Mbappé is well-known for each his first-rate competencies on the sector and his fantastic man or woman off it. Off the area, Mbappé is a modest and committed person who has obtained many admirers' hearts every as a soccer participant and as a role version for more youthful aspirant sportsmen. The following describe Kylian Mbappé in his off-location sports activities sports:

1. Humanitarian Initiatives: Kylian Mbappé has demonstrated a splendid self-control to improving society and helping those in want. He has participated in some of humanitarian responsibilities, supporting companies like kid's hospitals, underserved neighborhoods, and terrible kids pursue their desires of going to high school and collaborating in sports.

2. Youth Role Model: As a budding soccer big call, Mbappé is aware of his energy over more youthful supporters. He tries to offer an brilliant example for the following technology and takes this interest notably. He encourages others to pursue their aspirations and change the area by way of way of manner of hammering domestic the

price of perseverance, hard artwork, and devotion.

three. Family-oriented: Despite his notoriety and achievement, Kylian keeps a close to relationship alongside with his circle of relatives and acknowledges the impact they have got had on his existence. The beliefs his dad and mom and brothers instilled in him have helped him be successful each on and rancid the pitch, and he regularly mentions them with affection.

Mbappé is renowned for his sportsmanship and recognize for the game of soccer. Four. Respect for the Game. He is the epitome of sincere play and constantly treats his teammates and warring parties with appreciate. Fans, teammates, and coaches have all praised his behavior on and off the sector.

five. Academic Interests: Mbappé is interested in instructional pastimes further to his sports sports activities career.

Insisting at the want of a nicely-rounded education, he has been noticed urging more youthful gamers to combine their love of athletics with scholastic endeavors.

6. Positivity: Mbappé's incredible outlook and contagious grin make him a fave amongst fans anywhere. He famous resilience and a will to be successful by means of the usage of managing success and failure with grace.

7. Fashion & Style: Mbappé is famend for his elegant and complex appearances off the arena. He has demonstrated his love in fashion and fashion through taking component in plenty of of favor campaigns and sports.

eight. Diverse Cultural Background: Mbappé hails from a multicultural circle of relatives; his mother is Algerian and French and his father is Cameroonian. His tolerant and open-minded mind-set on lifestyles is a result of his cosmopolitan historical past.

Overall, Kylian Mbappé offers himself as a honest, charitable man who uses his characteristic to beautify the lives of others. People of each age live inspired by means of him because of his individual and actual effect at the globe, further to his football abilties.

nine:1 Mbappe's Charity Work and Social Initiatives

Kylian Mbappe participated in a number of social causes and charitable endeavors. Here are a a number of the humanitarian endeavors and sports activities sports for which he have turn out to be well-known:

1. "Inspired through KM" Charity Campaign: Kylian Mbappe started out his very very very own charity initiative to beneficial resource children with illnesses and impairments. The marketing advertising marketing campaign dreams to elevate coins and attention for a number of troubles affecting the health and welfare of kids.

2. Contributions to Non-Profit Organizations: Mbappe has a history of making big contributions to nonprofits that cope with social, health, and educational challenges impacting kids and teens. These contributions have supported projects which encompass building schools, providing scientific useful beneficial resource, and developing instructional get right of access to.

three. UNICEF Goodwill Ambassador: Kylian Mbappe changed into named a UNICEF Goodwill Ambassador in 2018. In this ability, he applied his notoriety and platform to sell children's rights and useful aid UNICEF's obligations to provide health, schooling, and protection to children in some unspecified time in the future of the arena who are in want.

4. Support for Sports and Education Programs: In addition to turning into a soccer sensation, Mbappe has demonstrated manual for initiatives that

help underprivileged youngsters via sports activities and education. He has taken thing in projects that help athletics as a device of real increase and empowerment for children from disadvantaged homes.

5. Charity Games and sports activities activities: To help some of reasons, Mbappe has taken detail in charity soccer video video games and activities. Football stars and one of a kind well-known human beings are frequently present at those activities, and the coins raised is given to charitable motives.

6. Disaster Relief Efforts: Kylian Mbappe has established his guide by way of way of assisting with treatment efforts at instances of herbal disasters or humanitarian crises. He has recommended human beings to help human beings impacted with the aid of using similar occurrences with the aid of the use of the use of his platform.

7. Use of Social Media: Mbappe has made use of his on-line presence to promote some of social issues and enlighten enthusiasts about the humanitarian organizations he backs. His massive fan base aids in amplifying the messages and growing their advantage.

9:2 Life Beyond Football

Kylian Mbappé's life is characterised via masses of pastimes and pastimes out of doors of football, in addition to a choice to have a nice have an impact on on society. Here are a few sides of his life that are not associated with football:

1. Academic Efforts: Mbappé prioritizes his studies and highbrow improvement at the same time as pursuing his football career. He has probably tried to strike a balance amongst his academic and carrying obligations, perhaps searching into subjects that hobby him.

2. Entrepreneurship: Mbappé might also moreover moreover have entered the commercial enterprise field given his notoriety and effect. He may have tried to installation himself as an entrepreneur and create a long-lasting financial empire thru sponsorships, investments, or developing his personal emblem.

3. Philanthropy and Charity Work: Mbappé is probably concerned in philanthropy and charity artwork, similar to he does on the sector. He may have began out out his very very own nonprofit organisation or worked with already-gift ones to reinforce quite a few issues, at the aspect of social welfare, education, and children's rights.

4. Style and Lifestyle: Mbappé is well identified for his experience of style and his love of fashion, and he can also have pursued this passion similarly. He may want to have worked with designers, launched his very very personal apparel line, or been lively within the fashion company.

5. Personal Growth and Development: Mbappé might be devoted to his non-public personal improvement similarly to his professional accomplishments. This can entail analyzing, traveling, or following pastimes that permit him to widen his horizons and deepen his lifestyles evaluations.

6. Family and Relationships: Mbappé locations a excessive fee on his tight ties to his own family. In addition to soccer, he may additionally moreover spend time along along with his loved ones, fostering and valuing the bonds which have helped him grow to be the man or woman he is nowadays.

7. Sports Advocacy and Promotion: Mbappé, a sports activities activities sports activities celeb, would possibly actively promote sports sports on numerous tiers, specially amongst younger humans. He ought to promote the price of sports activities in

promoting willpower, teamwork, and personal improvement.

eight. Public Speaking and Influencing: Given his appeal and recognition, Mbappé need to take part in sports and sports that want public talking. His realistic advice, shifting recollections, and inspirational messages also can inspire and encourage audiences everywhere.

9. Personal Fitness and Health: Mbappé in all likelihood places a excessive precedence on his fitness and health, just like any other expert athlete. In addition to soccer workout, he can also moreover have a look at distinctive physical interests and sports activities sports to hold his great well-being.

10. Creative Activities: Mbappé is pretty modern, as visible by the use of using his deft footwork on the football pitch. Off the sphere, he have to unique his imaginitive component through an entire lot of sports

activities, along with appearing, painting, and song.

While facts of Kylian Mbappé's existence out of doors of soccer stay unknown, it's far clean that he is a complicated man or woman with some of pastimes and a honest preference to make a difference in the worldwide. Mbappé's life adventure some distance from the football difficulty is in all likelihood to be full of achievement and which means that, whether or not or now not thru charitable pastime, company endeavors, or non-public improvement.

Chapter 9: Challenges And Setback

Kylian Mbappé, the French expert footballer, had already executed excellent achievement in his career. However, it is vital to word that the information provided proper right here might not encompass sports that occurred after September 2021. Here are a number of the worrying conditions and setbacks that Kylian Mbappé faced within the path of his career as much as that problem:

1. **Early Career Struggles:** Like many young gamers, Mbappé faced demanding situations in his early football profession. He had to paintings hard to face out amongst his buddies and stable a gap in pinnacle-level youngsters groups.

2. **Pressure and Expectations:** As a more youthful skills with large ability, Mbappé confronted vast stress and expectancies from fanatics, media, and football pundits. Living as plenty as such

expectancies may be overwhelming for any participant.

three. **Injuries:** Throughout his profession, Mbappé has had to deal with injuries that in short sidelined him and affected his overall performance on the world. Injuries are a commonplace setback in sports and can disrupt a player's rhythm and shape.

4. **Competition for Spots:** Playing for top-tier golf equipment like AS Monaco, Paris Saint-Germain (PSG), and the French countrywide institution technique fierce opposition for beginning spots. Mbappé had to compete with amazing talented gamers for his role within the lineup.

five. **Transfer Speculations:** Rumors and speculations surrounding functionality transfers to exclusive clubs also can create distractions and uncertainties for game enthusiasts. During his time at PSG, there had been ongoing speculations about Mbappé's future.

6. **Criticism and Media Scrutiny:** Being a excessive-profile participant, Mbappé faced scrutiny from the media and critics. Even minor dips in form or normal performance ought to enchantment to terrible attention, affecting his confidence and recognition.

7. **Handling Fame:** With remarkable achievement comes recognition, and managing surprising stardom at a young age may be hard. Maintaining a balanced private existence and specializing in football amidst the distractions of recognition isn't always usually smooth.

eight. **Big Match Pressure:** As one of the worldwide's notable footballers, Mbappé emerge as frequently tasked with handing over pinnacle performances in crucial suits, collectively with home and international competitions. The pressure of performing on the huge level can be excessive.

Despite those traumatic situations and setbacks, Kylian Mbappé has proven awesome resilience and resolution, overcoming barriers to turn out to be one of the brightest stars in international soccer.

10:1 Dealing with Injuries and setback

Throughout his expert profession, Kylian Mbappé needed to deal with a few massive setbacks and injuries. Please be aware that any events or enhancements that passed off after that date won't be covered on this fabric. Here are some times of Kylian Mbappé overcoming hurdles and injuries:

Injury to the ankle (July 2019): Mbappé sustained a extensive ankle harm on July 27, 2019, at the same time as gambling against Saint-Étienne inside the French Cup very last. The harm changed right into a massive blow because it introduced approximately him to miss some essential Paris Saint-

Germain (PSG) video games and brought on uncertainty over his availability for upcoming contests.

2. Knee Injury (February 2020) Mbappé suffered a thigh harm in a in form in opposition to Montpellier in February 2020. He turn out to be sidelined for some weeks with the beneficial aid of the harm, which became terrible information for PSG because they have been taking element in every nearby and European championships.

3. (September 2020) COVID-19 Diagnosis: In September 2020, Mbappé tested notable for COVID-19, like many sportsmen all around the worldwide. His suit fitness and schooling suffered due to having to isolate himself and pass over a couple of suits.

four. Calf Damage (May 2021) Just some weeks earlier than the UEFA Champions League semifinal healthful against Manchester City in May 2021, Mbappé sustained a calf harm. Though he modified into capable to participate inside the second leg no matter the harm, he have become no longer capable of prevent PSG from dropping the in form and missing out on the championship.

Any athlete who reviews an harm should possibly locate it hard to address it psychologically and bodily, however Kylian Mbappé has examined he can get better from setbacks and perform at his great. In order to get thru these trying instances, he has relied on the help of his group's scientific employees, his non-public self-control to restoration, and his ability for optimism. It's important to don't forget that setbacks and accidents are a everyday part of a professional athlete's career, and the way they are treated and recovered from might also affect how successful they will be in the game in the long run.

10:2 Handling Expectations and Pressure

Given his first-rate potential and quick ascent to recognition, Kylian Mbappé's football career has blanketed a terrific amount of managing strain and expectations. Here is how he has treated the tremendous stress and expectations for the duration of his profession:

1. Mindfulness and Concentration Mbappé has a powerful mind-set and a laser-like cognizance on his workout. He is conscious that meeting out of doors necessities is a critical difficulty of turning into a top-tier athlete and chooses to reputation on his development and average basic overall performance in preference to succumb to the pressure.

2. Self-perception in Capabilities: Mbappé's self notion in his skills is important for handling expectancies. He is confident in his capabilities because of the reality he is privy to his competencies, which permits him to stand hard situations and issues with a excellent outlook.

3. Strong Support System: For Mbappé, having a network of buddies, own family, coaches, and teammates has been vital. They provide him assist, course, and information as he gives with the desires of the soccer worldwide.

4. Role fashions and mentoring Mbappé has mentioned the significance of mentors and pro athletes in his lifestyles. He income perspective and manages immoderate expectations thru taking note of older gamers' memories and looking for steerage from human beings who've prolonged past thru comparable conditions.

five. Accepting Challenges: Instead of heading off strain, Mbappé welcomes it and perspectives it as an possibility to make bigger every as a participant and someone. He can perform at his high-quality even in immoderate-stakes circumstances because to his comfortable outlook.

6. Managing Your Personal Life While Playing Football: For addressing expectancies, it's far vital to keep a healthy stability among football and personal life. Mbappé schedules non-football-related sports activities, which continues him grounded and revitalized.

Media Management: Mbappé and his personnel have taken the initiative to manipulate media publicity and make certain he isn't always overshadowed via it. He can focus on his sport with out being distracted through way of a few element because of this approach.

8. Maintaining Humility: Mbappé has maintained his modesty and grounding regardless of his notable achievement. He is conscious that football is a fixed pastime and thanks his teammates and coaches for helping him be successful.

9. Concentrating on Long-Term Objectives: Mbappé concentrates on his prolonged-

term football dreams and goals in desire to becoming distracted with the useful resource of way of expectations and hoopla which can be really brief. His ability to region subjects in attitude and keep a ordinary artwork ethic is aided with the useful resource of this angle.

Being able to address stress and expectancies with maturity and poise speaks volumes approximately Kylian Mbappé's individual and highbrow fortitude. He keeps to growth as one of the wonderful soccer game enthusiasts in the international by means of keeping a balanced approach and being dependable to his ideals.

Chapter 10: The Next Generation

Eleven:1 Motivating Future Footballers

The French football celebrity Kylian Mbappe has captivated the globe collectively with his fantastic understanding, approach, and tenacity. He labored assiduously to recognize his dreams of being a football movie superstar beginning at a younger age. His inspirational story conjures up masses more youthful game enthusiasts all over the global to chase their goals and in no way surrender on their aspirations.

1. Strive hard, dream huge:

The cost of having incredible dreams and tasty in hard desires is emphasized through Mbappe's tale. He had aspirations of being one of the global's pinnacle football game enthusiasts as a more youthful infant. He knew that having desires could now not be enough, so he made a willpower to taking walks difficult, going via rigorous education, and normally improving his capabilities.

Young football players ought to research this lesson for them and understand that everything is viable with difficult artwork and resolution.

2. Accept Challenges

Mbappe overcame many issues and hurdles for the duration of his profession, but he by no means gave up. Instead, he saw these problems as possibilities to beautify. Mbappe used those reviews to make bigger as a player and a person, whether or not or not it come to be managing up in the direction of more professional fighters or dealing with the strain of important video video video games. Football gamers of their early years must view difficulties as opportunities to increase and increase.

3. Consistency Pays Off:

Mbappe encountered obstacles along the manner to fulfillment. Along the street, he had setbacks and disappointments, but he in no way out of area need in himself. He did not allow disasters outline him; rather, he exploited them to gasoline his resiliency. Young soccer gamers ought to apprehend that obstacles are a everyday a part of any route, but that tenacity and resiliency are what ultimately result in fulfillment.

4. Work as a Team: Mbappe prioritizes collaboration above the entirety else, however his extremely good character skills. He is aware that soccer is a group game and that fulfillment relies upon on cooperation amongst teammates. Young football gamers should understand the rate of teamwork, verbal exchange, and mutual resource each on and rancid the pitch. Being a group participant improves no longer simply an individual's overall performance but moreover that of the entire business enterprise.

five. Remain Humble and Grounded: Despite incomes reputation and fulfillment on a global scale, Mbappe has enormously maintained his humility and grounding. He continues to cope with human beings with recognize and decency irrespective of his success. Young gamers want to be privy to his humility and hold in thoughts that right greatness is a fabricated from each capabilities and personal individual.

Numerous more youthful footballers in some unspecified time in the future of the arena are stimulated through the usage of Kylian Mbappe's ascent to football achievement. Every potential football player should model their artwork ethic, tenacity, humility, and resolution after him. Young athletes need to emulate Mbappe's achievement with the aid of setting lofty goals, strolling difficult, accepting obstacles, and setting a excessive cost on collaboration. Keep in mind that the whole lot begins with a dream and the choice to make it come real.

11:2 Impact on the Youth and Grassroots Football

The have an effect on Kylian Mbappe has had on younger human beings and grassroots soccer is not anything quick of splendid. Mbappe, one of the most well-known soccer gamers within the worldwide, has inspired and supported younger gamers on the grassroots level by using the usage of the use of his platform and affect, growing a long-lasting imprint on the upcoming crop of soccer data.

1. Motivating younger athletes:

Mbappe's course as a more youthful footballer who have grow to be famous at a younger age serves for example for aspiring footballers anywhere in the international. Kids from all backgrounds look as a good buy as him as a position version due to the truth he exemplifies how attempt, tenacity, and a love of the sport can reason knowledge one's goals. Young athletes are stimulated with the aid of his accomplishment to believe in themselves and pursue their targets with unyielding tenacity.

2. Promoting Inclusion and Diversity:

Being a famend participant of African history like Mbappe has aided in advancing inclusion and range in soccer. He stands as a testament to the truth that knowledge is privy to no bounds and that gambling football can unite humans from many origins and cultures. His have an effect on on teens football gamers in the direction of the arena conjures up splendor and team spirit off the pitch as well.

three. Community-based Initiatives

Mbappe has actively subsidized grassroots soccer obligations and agencies that prioritize fostering new ability. He appreciates the price of investment children development initiatives that offer children with low earning the hazard to use pinnacle-notch facilities and training. By assisting the ones programs, Mbappe makes excellent that information is advanced on the grassroots degree and encourages greater younger gamers to look at their objectives of playing football.

four. Volunteering:

Mbappe has participated in a number of humanitarian initiatives that useful resource kids and underprivileged organizations further to his contributions to grassroots obligations. He makes a widespread difference in the lives of severa younger humans with the resource of donating his movie famous person and riches to businesses that enhance healthcare, schooling, and sports sports.

5. Motivating the Next Wave of French Footballers:

Mbappe's accomplishments as a member of the French national group and a sizeable contributor to their victory have rekindled more youthful enthusiasm in soccer in France. In an attempt to emulate their idols, an increasing number of more youthful gamers are getting a member of community teams and academies around the united states of the us. The bar for greater younger French footballers has been lifted with the resource of Mbappe's fulfillment, inspiring others to goal excessive.

6. Supporting Fair Play and Respect: Mbappe is renowned for his sportsmanship and understand for opponents similarly to his football talents. Young gamers may additionally analyze from his behavior each on and off the sphere with the aid of highlighting the value of sincere play and admire for the sport, splendid gamers, coaches, and spectators.

The have an effect on Kylian Mbappe has had at the kids and grassroots football scene is going past soccer. He has improved younger athletes all the world over together collectively together with his inspirational course, humanitarian giving, and advocacy for range and inclusion. Mbappe guarantees that the future of football is exquisite and entire of potential with the aid of the usage of aggressively assisting grassroots initiatives and developing skills at its foundations. He remains seemed as a lot as thru more youthful game enthusiasts, and his legacy will simply have an effect at the future soccer stars.

Chapter 11: Looking Ahead

The prospects for Kylian Mbappe's destiny as a soccer participant are charming as he develops and grows as a participant. Here are a few future factors for the burgeoning French celebrity to consider:

1. Peak of His Powers: Mbappe stays in his early to mid-20s on the time of writing, this means that he has no longer yet reached the years of his profession at the same time as he's at his incredible. He will in all likelihood be at the top of his physical and cerebral powers even as he hits his past due

20s and early 30s, making him a good greater fearsome stress on the sector.

2. Potential Transfers: Given his remarkable potential and power, Mbappe may be related to moves to different elite European teams. Despite being an vital member of Paris Saint-Germain, he can search for clean disturbing conditions and research in different competitions. A high-profile circulate might also alter his career's route and introduce him to new footballing situations.

3. Pursuit of Individual prizes: Mbappe is a exquisite candidate for several character prizes, alongside aspect the Ballon d'Or, way to his splendid achievements. He stands out as one of the maximum versatile strikers in the sport way to his capability to advantage goals and open up opportunities for his teammates. The acclaim and plaudits are in all likelihood going to come back so long as he continues acting well in every america and Europe.

4. UEFA Champions League Glory: Despite supporting PSG reap the championship sport, Mbappe has but to win the Champions League. He will actually be focused on the destiny and eager to win the coveted opposition and cement his region among the best soccer players in statistics. He in spite of the reality that has his points of interest set on triumphing the Champions League with PSG or a few other group.

5. Leadership Role: As Mbappe acquires understanding and authority, he may additionally additionally logically pass right into a management function each on and off the arena. He can encourage and encourage more youthful game enthusiasts collectively together with his extraordinary skills and art work ethic, serving as an example for the approaching generation of footballers.

6. International Success: Mbappe might be traumatic to characteristic additional global titles to his series after experiencing World Cup victory with France in 2018. His love for

Les Bleus will never fade, and assisting his country gain further victories will continually come first.

7. Legacy: Mbappe is probably acutely aware of his legacy as his career develops. Beyond his on-discipline successes, he has the capability to symbolize the sport as an envoy via using his feature to clearly have an impact on a number of societal issues and inspire aspiring athletes everywhere in the worldwide.

In quit, Kylian Mbappe has a promising future ahead of him. The footballing worldwide anxiously anticipates the upcoming chapters in his splendid journey as he keeps to increase his abilities, draw schooling from his errors, and set new goals. He has the capability to influence the sport for many years to go lower back and make a long lasting have an effect on on the game thanks to his skills, enthusiasm, and devotion.

12:1 Mbappe's Future Goals and Ambitions

One can splendid assume about Kylian Mbappé's lengthy-time period dreams and aspirations. But judging on his preceding remarks and movements, it is viable that he aspires to a number of the topics indexed beneath:

1. Continue to acquire fulfillment at Paris Saint-Germain (PSG): Mbappé has loved success at PSG, in which he has received severa domestic championships and examined off his brilliance at the European scene. One of his number one dreams may be to help the group maintain its achievement and win more UEFA Champions League and Ligue 1 championships.

2. Winning the UEFA Champions League: Mbappé has already lengthy long gone near engaging in this feat with both AS Monaco and PSG. The UEFA Champions League is the maximum prestigious club opposition in

European football. He probably has a burning choice to win the trophy and installation himself as one of the all-time greats.

three. Winning More Individual Awards: As a expert player, Mbappé likely desires to take domestic extra man or woman honors, such as the Ballon d'Or. He has already been nominated for the coveted prize and hopes to finish his career due to the fact the top player in the international.

4. Success with the French National squad: After helping France win the 2018 FIFA World Cup, Mbappé might be involved to help the squad in protective its identify in upcoming competitions. He will preserve to have a sturdy preference to compete for his country at prestigious worldwide sports just like the World Cup and the European Championship.

5. Make a Name for Yourself in Several Leagues: Despite Mbappé's splendid

achievement in Ligue 1, he may furthermore want to installation himself in unique elite competitions similar to the English Premier League, La Liga, or Serie A. At a while in his career, he may additionally want to replace to a brand new league.

6. Persevere in Your Personal Development: Mbappé is renowned for his fantastic art work ethic and ambition to constantly get higher as a player. His desire to decorate and hone his abilities will probable fuel him sooner or later of his profession.

7. Give Back to the Community: Mbappé has taken detail in community carrier initiatives and charity endeavors off the pitch. It is probably that he is going to keep on using his role and accomplishments to decorate society.

12:2 Legacy in Football

The impact Kylian Mbappé has had on football is superb. Mbappé became famous as one of the maximum gifted and exciting younger soccer game enthusiasts of his generation after being born on December 20, 1998, in Bondy, a suburb of Paris, France. Both on and off the sphere, he has had a big effect on the sport.

1. Awe-Inspiring Talent Mbappé proven a herbal know-how for walking at breakneck speeds, gliding beyond defenders effects, and completing with amazing poise from an early age. His technical skills, vision, and capability to attain goals led him comparisons to some of the high-quality game enthusiasts within the records of the game.

2. Early Achievement with AS Monaco: Mbappé's large wreck as a expert got here with AS Monaco inside the 2016–2017 advertising and marketing advertising marketing campaign. He changed into instrumental in the agency's Ligue 1 championship and run to the UEFA Champions League semifinals. As a surrender quit end result of his exceptional

accomplishments, he received the Golden Boy award, which honors the finest young player in Europe.

three. World Cup victory: Due to his great fashionable standard performance at the 2018 FIFA World Cup, Mbappé's call will bypass down in football statistics all of the time. He emerge as a crucial part of the French countrywide squad after they acquired their 2d World Cup. He won the match's Best Young Player award for his explosive tempo and vital goals, and he have end up a instance of the team's younger excitement and offensive electricity.

4. Relentless Excellence Mbappé maintained his fulfillment at Paris Saint-Germain (PSG) after the World Cup victory, while he displayed his functionality to perform at the maximum critical structures. He dominated Ligue 1, incomes severa national championships and character honors,

consisting of because the Ligue 1 Player of the Year trophy.

5. Champion's Mentality: Mbappé has constantly installed a prevailing mind-set and a preference to do higher. He always seeks to beautify himself and pushes himself to emerge as the pleasant model of himself.

6. Role model and deliver of belief Mbappé is a characteristic version for aspiring football game enthusiasts all around the global due to his humble character and strength of will to his artwork, in addition to his on-vicinity accomplishments. He uses his role to inspire and inspire others, in particular greater younger human beings, by way of manner of displaying how staying power and tough strive can result in success.

(7) Global Icon The recognition of Mbappé is felt well beyond undertaking. One of the most famous and marketable sportsmen on

the globe, he has grow to be a cultural icon through endorsing massive agencies and performing on magazine covers.

8. Keeping the Legacy Alive As he overcame new barriers and reached new career milestones, his legacy might actually hold to change.

Kylian Mbappé's legacy in soccer might be defined with the aid of the use of the use of his terrific expertise, his victories on the biggest degrees, and his have an effect on as a feature version and idea to masses of hundreds of human beings. He has made an extended lasting impact on football and may be recognized as one of the first-class players of his time as one among the game's largest stars.

Chapter 12: Early Life And Football Beginnings

The more youthful Frenchman has taken the arena with the beneficial aid of hurricane along along together with his lightning-speedy pace, splendid capability, and herbal capacity to achieve goals. But in which did all of it begin for this footballing prodigy? In this essay, we will explore Kylian Mbappe's youth and football beginnings, from his youth in Bondy to his upward push to recognition with AS Monaco.

Kylian Mbappe emerge as born on December 20th, 1998, in Bondy, a suburb of Paris. His parents, Wilfried Mbappe and Fayza Lamari, each have roots in Africa - Wilfried is from Cameroon even as Fayza is of Algerian descent. Kylian grew up in a multicultural environment, surrounded by using unique languages, cultures, and traditions. This severa upbringing may later play a big function in shaping his person and outlook on existence.

From an early age, Kylian showed a keen hobby in football. His father, Wilfried, emerge as a teenagers educate at AS Bondy, a nearby football membership in their network. Wilfried diagnosed his son's capabilities early on and started out training him at the age of four. Kylian rapid developed a love for the game and spent most of his formative years gambling football within the streets along together with his buddies.

Despite his apparent skills, Kylian faced many challenges in his early years. Bondy modified into a tough network, and the younger footballer had to overcome many obstacles to pursue his goals. He regularly performed on makeshift pitches with out a grass, and the situations had been an prolonged manner from exceptional. However, this did now not deter Kylian from pursuing his passion for soccer.

As he grew older, Kylian's knowledge have become more apparent. He joined the youngsters academy at AS Bondy and fast hooked up himself as one of the most promising gamers in the club. His pace, agility, and technical functionality stuck the eye of scouts from several top golf equipment in Europe.

In 2013, on the identical time as Kylian have end up simply 14 years vintage, he turned into invited to strive out for the children academy at Clairefontaine, the brilliant French Football Federation's countrywide training center. The academy is understood for producing some of France's awesome footballers, which includes Thierry Henry, Nicolas Anelka, and Kylian's idol, Zinedine Zidane. Kylian inspired the coaches at Clairefontaine together with his competencies and have become furnished an area in the academy.

Kylian's time at Clairefontaine changed into a turning element in his career. He knowledgeable with some of the exceptional young game enthusiasts in

France and received world-beauty training from professional specialists. He furthermore advanced a sturdy art work ethic and subject, which would possibly serve him nicely in his destiny career.

In 2015, Kylian signed for AS Monaco's teenagers academy. Monaco end up a membership at the rise, having just been promoted to Ligue 1, France's pinnacle branch. Kylian rapid installation himself as one of the maximum promising game enthusiasts inside the academy and turned into speedy promoted to the primary crew.

Kylian made his debut for AS Monaco in December 2015, at the age of 16. He got here on as an opportunity in a league healthful inside the direction of Caen and right now made an impact, scoring his first motive for the membership. This made him the youngest-ever scorer for AS Monaco and the youngest player to attain in Ligue 1 given that 1974.

Kylian's performances for AS Monaco fast stuck the eye of pinnacle golf equipment at some stage in Europe. In 2017, he helped lead Monaco to the Ligue 1 name and the semifinals of the UEFA Champions League. His performances in Europe's satisfactory club opposition had been in particular sudden, as he scored six dreams in six video video video games towards some of the continent's exceptional agencies.

In the summer time of 2017, Kylian changed into scenario to intense switch hypothesis. Several top golf equipment, in conjunction with Real Madrid, Barcelona, and Manchester City, had been reportedly interested in signing the younger Frenchman. However, it became Paris Saint-Germain (PSG) who in the long run received the race for his signature, signing him on mortgage with an choice to buy for a rate of €one hundred eighty million.

Kylian's flow into to PSG changed right into a sizeable second in his profession. He joined a crew that had without a doubt acquired 4 consecutive Ligue 1 titles and changed into on the lookout for to set up itself as truely one in every of Europe's pinnacle clubs. Kylian rapid set up himself as a key participant for PSG, forming a lethal partnership with fellow celebrity Neymar and predominant the organization to every other Ligue 1 select out.

Kylian's performances for PSG were now not something brief of superb. He has scored over 100 dreams for the membership in handiest over three seasons, supporting them win three Ligue 1 titles and achieve the final of the UEFA Champions League in 2020. He has additionally acquired numerous man or woman awards, which encompass the Golden Boy award in 2017 and the Ligue 1 Player of the Year award in 2018 and 2019.

Kylian's fulfillment on the pitch has no longer lengthy past neglected off the field. He is considerably seemed as one of the most marketable athletes in the global, with numerous excessive-profile endorsement offers and sponsorships. He is also mentioned for his philanthropic paintings, having donated his complete World Cup bonus to charity and released his non-public foundation to guide underprivileged children.

Kylian Mbappe's teens and soccer beginnings are a testament to his abilties, difficult art work, and resolution. From playing soccer within the streets of Bondy to becoming one of the global's extremely good gamers at PSG, Kylian has conquer many boundaries to gain his dreams. His tale is an idea to younger footballers round the world and a reminder that some issue is possible with determination and perseverance.

MBAPPE'S YOUTH CAREER

Kylian Mbappe is a footballing prodigy, a player who has taken the arena by way of way of typhoon alongside together with his tremendous information, lightning-rapid tempo, and natural capability to gain dreams. While his childhood has been explored in-depth, it's miles his kids career that without a doubt showcases the making of a phenom. From his days at AS Bondy to his upward push to fame with AS Monaco, Kylian's adventure to turning into one of the worldwide's amazing game enthusiasts come to be marked by way of the use of hard paintings, determination, and a persevering with pursuit of excellence.

Kylian's youngsters career started at AS Bondy, a close-by soccer membership in his community. His father, Wilfried Mbappe, changed into a teenagers teach at the club and identified his son's skills early on. He began education Kylian on the age of four, and the young footballer brief evolved a love for the sport. Despite going via many annoying situations in his early years, together with playing on makeshift pitches without a grass, Kylian's ardour for soccer never wavered.

As he grew older, Kylian's understanding have emerge as greater apparent. He joined the youngsters academy at AS Bondy and speedy established himself as one of the maximum promising gamers inside the membership. His pace, agility, and technical capability stuck the attention of scouts from numerous pinnacle golf equipment in Europe.

In 2013, Kylian became invited to attempt out for the children academy at Clairefontaine, the outstanding French Football Federation's country wide education center. The academy is concept for producing a number of France's exceptional footballers, which incorporates Thierry Henry, Nicolas Anelka, and Kylian's idol, Zinedine Zidane. Kylian impressed the coaches at Clairefontaine along together with his capabilities and became provided an area within the academy.

Kylian's time at Clairefontaine turn out to be a turning component in his profession. He educated with a number of the incredible younger gamers in France and purchased global-elegance training from skilled experts. He additionally superior a robust work ethic and vicinity, which could possibly serve him properly in his destiny career.

In 2015, Kylian signed for AS Monaco's youngsters academy. Monaco have become a membership on the upward push, having absolutely been promoted to Ligue 1, France's pinnacle department. Kylian quick installation himself as one of the most promising gamers inside the academy and modified into fast promoted to the primary group.

Kylian made his debut for AS Monaco in December 2015, at the age of sixteen. He came on as an alternative in a league fit in opposition to Caen and right now made an effect, scoring his first purpose for the membership. This made him the youngest-ever scorer for AS Monaco and the youngest player to obtain in Ligue 1 because 1974.

Kylian's performances for AS Monaco quickly caught the attention of top clubs at some stage in Europe. In 2017, he helped lead Monaco to the Ligue 1 name and the semifinals of the UEFA Champions League. His performances in Europe's maximum exceptional club competition have been specially brilliant, as he scored six desires in six video games in opposition to a number of the continent's great groups.

Kylian's upward thrust to repute changed into now not without its annoying conditions. He confronted criticism from some quarters for his perceived loss of physicality and defensive art work price. However, he remained focused on his endeavor and endured to paintings difficult on his weaknesses.

One of Kylian's defining moments came within the 2018 FIFA World Cup. He performed a pivotal characteristic in France's triumph, scoring 4 dreams in seven video video games and prevailing the occasion's Best Young Player award. His performances on the World Cup cemented his recognition as one of the worldwide's terrific gamers and sparked renewed interest from top golf equipment for the duration of Europe.

In 2018, Kylian signed for Paris Saint-Germain (PSG) in a deal well well well worth €a hundred 80 million, making him the second one-maximum highly-priced player in information on the time. His bypass to PSG have become a big 2d in his profession, as he joined a group that had just received four consecutive Ligue 1 titles and modified into on the lookout for to set up itself as considered one among Europe's top golf equipment.

Kylian rapid established himself as a key player for PSG, forming a lethal partnership with fellow movie celebrity Neymar and vital the company to any other Ligue 1 name. His performances for PSG had been now not some issue quick of first-rate. He has scored over 100 dreams for the membership in only over three seasons, assisting them win 3 Ligue 1 titles and gain the final of the UEFA Champions League in 2020. He has also received numerous character awards, which include the Golden Boy award in 2017 and the Ligue 1 Player of the Year award in 2018 and 2019.

Kylian's fulfillment on the pitch has now not long long gone overlooked off the arena. He is broadly seemed as one of the maximum marketable athletes in the worldwide, with severa excessive-profile endorsement offers and sponsorships. He is likewise identified for his philanthropic artwork, having donated his complete World Cup bonus to charity and launched his very private basis to useful resource underprivileged youngsters.

Kylian Mbappe's kids career is a testomony to his talents, hard work, and determination. From his days at AS Bondy to his upward push to recognition with AS Monaco and PSG, Kylian has conquer many limitations to gain his desires. His story is an belief to young footballers spherical the sector and a reminder that something is viable with self-discipline and perseverance. As he maintains to enlarge and evolve as a participant, it's miles clear that Kylian Mbappe is destined for greatness.

Chapter 13: Mbappe's Meteoric Rise In As Monaco

The younger Frenchman Kylian Mbappe has taken the sport thru storm considering that making his expert debut for AS Monaco in 2015. He fast set up himself as one of the maximum promising gamers in Europe, and his meteoric rise to popularity has been now not a few factor quick of super.

Mbappe's time at AS Monaco grow to be marked with the aid of a series of file-breaking performances that cemented his recognition as one of the global's wonderful game enthusiasts. He broke numerous statistics in a few unspecified time within the destiny of his time on the club, together with becoming the youngest player to attain ten dreams in a unmarried season in Ligue 1. His outstanding form helped lead Monaco to the Ligue 1 understand in 2017, and he carried out a pivotal function of their run to the semifinals of the UEFA Champions League.

Mbappe's upward thrust to fame modified into no longer without its disturbing situations, however. He faced complaint from a few quarters for his perceived lack of physicality and defensive paintings charge. He additionally had to attend to the strain of being one of the most promising younger gamers in Europe and the expectations that came with it. Despite the ones traumatic conditions, Mbappe remained focused on his pastime and endured to art work hard on his weaknesses.

One of Mbappe's defining moments at AS Monaco got here in the 2016-2017 season. He scored 26 goals in all competitions, which encompass six in the Champions League, assisting Monaco reach the semifinals of the competition for the number one time because of the truth 2004. His performances earned him an area in the UEFA Champions League Squad of the Season, alongside some of the amazing game enthusiasts in Europe.

Mbappe's performances in Ligue 1 have been in addition sudden. He scored 15 goals in 29 league appearances, assisting Monaco win their first league discover considering 2000. His form earned him the Ligue 1 Young Player of the Year award, as well as an area within the Ligue 1 Team of the Season.

Mbappe's wonderful shape at AS Monaco caught the attention of top golf equipment during Europe. In 2017, he signed for Paris Saint-Germain (PSG) in a deal properly actually well worth €100 eighty million, making him the second one-maximum steeply-priced player in data at the time. His pass to PSG grow to be a big 2d in his career, as he joined a team that had sincerely won 4 consecutive Ligue 1 titles and became seeking to set up itself as one in every of Europe's pinnacle golf equipment.

Mbappe's time at PSG has been marked thru persevered achievement on the pitch.

He has fashioned a deadly partnership with fellow celeb Neymar and has helped lead PSG to a few Ligue 1 titles and the very last of the UEFA Champions League in 2020. Mbappe's performances for PSG were nothing quick of amazing. He has scored over 100 goals for the club in first-rate over three seasons, assisting them set up themselves as one of the first-rate companies in Europe.

Mbappe's success on the pitch has no longer prolonged long past left out off the arena. He is broadly appeared as one of the most marketable athletes in the worldwide, with numerous immoderate-profile endorsement offers and sponsorships. He is also acknowledged for his philanthropic artwork, having donated his complete World Cup bonus to charity and released his personal basis to guide underprivileged youngsters.

Mbappe's meteoric upward push in AS Monaco is a testament to his statistics, tough artwork, and resolution. He overcame numerous obstacles to acquire his goals and mounted himself as one of the best game enthusiasts in Europe at a young age. His story is an concept to younger footballers round the area and a reminder that some detail is feasible with determination and perseverance.

One of the most remarkable elements of Mbappe's upward push to recognition is his awesome tempo. He is notion for his lightning-rapid pace, which permits him to outrun defenders and create scoring opportunities for himself and his teammates. His pace is a stop stop result of years of hard art work and schooling, further to his natural capability.

Mbappe's pace modified into on entire show at some point of his time at AS Monaco. He broke the file for the quickest intention in Ligue 1 information in February 2017, scoring just 90 seconds proper right right into a suit in competition to SM Caen.

He additionally set a contemporary-day report for the fastest hat-trick in Ligue 1 history, scoring three desires in best thirteen minutes in competition to FC Metz in May 2018.

Mbappe's velocity has furthermore been a key element in his success at PSG. He has scored numerous goals with the resource of manner of the use of his tempo to conquer defenders and create scoring possibilities. His tempo has furthermore helped him end up one of the nice counter-attacking players within the global, as he is able to fast transition from defense to attack and create goalscoring possibilities for his group.

Another key problem in Mbappe's achievement at AS Monaco became his excellent finishing ability. He has a herbal expertise for scoring desires and has advanced a scientific aspect in the front of motive over the years. His completing capability become on whole show all through his time at Monaco, in which he scored severa goals with every feet and his head.

Mbappe's finishing capability has endured to enhance at PSG. He has scored numerous desires in lots of techniques, on the facet of prolonged-range moves, faucet-ins, and headers. His ability to achieve from all regions of the pitch makes him a constant hazard to opposing defenses and has helped him set up himself as one of the high-quality strikers inside the global.

Mbappe's paintings price and state of affairs have moreover been key factors in his achievement at AS Monaco. He is idea for his tireless art work ethic and his willingness to region within the difficult yards for his crew. His trouble on and rancid the pitch has additionally been excellent, as he has avoided any major disciplinary troubles all through his profession.

Mbappe's paintings rate and location have persevered to electrify at PSG. He is notion for his capacity to song again and guard at the same time as wanted, as well as his willingness to region within the tough yards for his team. His place on and off the pitch has furthermore been exemplary, as he has avoided any principal disciplinary troubles thinking about the reality that becoming a member of the membership.

Mbappe's meteoric upward thrust in AS Monaco became a defining 2d in his profession. He established himself as one of the terrific more younger players in Europe and broke numerous records along the way. His success at AS Monaco paved the way for his circulate to PSG, in which he has continued to establish himself as one of the awesome game enthusiasts in the worldwide.

Chapter 14: Mbappe's Triumph With The French National Team

Kylian Mbappe's fulfillment on the club level became fast found with the useful resource of his inclusion in the French national team. He made his debut for Les Bleus in 2017 and quick have emerge as a key participant for the group. His performances helped France win the 2018 FIFA World Cup, cementing his fame as one of the top notch gamers in the global.

Mbappe's triumph with the French countrywide group changed into the culmination of years of difficult artwork and electricity of will. He had usually dreamed of playing for France and representing his u . S . A . On the world level. His performances inside the World Cup had been now not whatever short of awesome, as he scored 4 desires in seven fits and became named the match's Best Young Player.

Mbappe's performances in the World Cup were a testomony to his super knowledge, hard paintings, and backbone. He overcame numerous obstacles to gain his dreams and established himself as one of the brilliant game enthusiasts in the global. His story is an idea to more younger footballers spherical the arena and a reminder that a few thing is feasible with self-control and perseverance.

Mbappe's World Cup journey began in the agency degree, in which he performed a pivotal feature in France's development to the knockout rounds. He scored his first World Cup intention in France's 2d institution degree healthful closer to Peru, assisting Les Bleus solid a 1-zero victory. He additionally supplied an assist in France's final organisation diploma in form in the direction of Denmark, which caused a 0-zero draw.

Mbappe's performances inside the knockout rounds were even more first rate. He scored two dreams in France's Round of 16 fit in opposition to Argentina, together with a lovable solo try that showcased his amazing tempo and capacity. His performance helped France sturdy a 4-three victory and enhance to the quarterfinals.

In the quarterfinals, Mbappe was yet again instrumental in France's victory. He furnished an assist for Raphael Varane's beginning aim in France's 2-zero victory over Uruguay. His pace and potential added on troubles for Uruguay's safety in the path of the healthy, and he became named Man of the Match for his standard overall performance.

Mbappe's semifinal common standard overall performance in competition to Belgium have become one of the highlights of the occasion. He changed into a consistent hazard to Belgium's protection, using his tempo and ability to create numerous scoring possibilities for himself and his teammates. He also furnished an help for Samuel Umtiti's prevailing aim, supporting France steady a 1-zero victory and enhance to the final.

In the final, Mbappe yet again confirmed why he is one of the top notch gamers in the global. He modified into a ordinary risk to Croatia's protection, the use of his tempo and talent to create severa scoring opportunities for himself and his teammates. He additionally gained a penalty inside the first half of of, which Antoine Griezmann converted to provide France the lead. Mbappe's basic usual performance helped France stable a 4-2 victory and win their 2nd World Cup call.

Mbappe's performances inside the World Cup earned him numerous accolades. He changed into named the event's Best Young Player, turning into the youngest player to win the award due to the fact its inception in 2006. He changed into moreover included in the FIFA World Cup Dream Team, alongside a number of the first-rate game enthusiasts inside the worldwide.

Mbappe's triumph with the French country wide organization modified proper right into a defining second in his profession. He installation himself as one of the terrific gamers inside the global and cemented his recognition as a future movie celeb of the game. His performances inside the World Cup have been a testomony to his high-quality understanding, difficult art work, and resolution, and his tale is an proposal to more youthful footballers round the arena.

Mbappe's success with the French national group grow to be not without its demanding situations, however. He faced criticism from some quarters for his perceived loss of protective paintings fee and physicality. He additionally had to cope with the stress of gambling for one of the first rate groups inside the international and the expectations that came with it. Despite the ones challenges, Mbappe remained centered on his undertaking and persevered to artwork tough on his weaknesses.

One of Mbappe's defining moments inside the World Cup got here within the Round of 16 in shape in competition to Argentina. He scored desires in the fit, inclusive of a lovable solo try that showcased his brilliant pace and capacity. The purpose became paying homage to a number of the satisfactory goals in World Cup information and cemented Mbappe's popularity as a destiny movie star of the sport.

Mbappe's splendid pace become on entire show all through the in shape. He used his tempo to outrun defenders and create scoring opportunities for himself and his teammates. His velocity was a prevent end result of years of tough paintings and schooling, similarly to his herbal potential.

Mbappe's completing ability changed into moreover a key detail in France's achievement within the World Cup. He has a natural abilities for scoring goals and has evolved a scientific facet inside the the front of purpose through the years. His completing potential have become on complete display in the route of the match, as he scored four dreams in seven suits and helped France win their 2d World Cup name.

Mbappe's artwork price and area have been moreover key factors in France's fulfillment in the World Cup. He is concept for his tireless artwork ethic and his willingness to position in the hard yards for his organization. His discipline on and off the pitch come to be additionally exquisite, as he averted any most essential disciplinary troubles at a few stage inside the occasion.

Mbappe's triumph with the French national crew changed into a defining second in his profession. He installation himself as one of the terrific players inside the worldwide and cemented his repute as a destiny celebrity of the game. His performances within the World Cup had been a testomony to his awesome understanding, hard paintings, and determination, and his tale is an concept to younger footballers round the arena.

Kylian Mbappe's triumph with the French countrywide group inside the 2018 FIFA World Cup modified into a defining 2d in his career. He mounted himself as one of the nice game enthusiasts inside the international and cemented his popularity as a future movie star of the sport. His performances inside the World Cup had been not anything brief of sudden, as he scored four desires in seven suits and changed into named the healthy's Best Young Player. Mbappe's achievement with the French country wide organization have become a testament to his high-quality talent, difficult paintings, and resolution, and his tale is an idea to more youthful footballers spherical the vicinity.

Chapter 15: Mbappe's Transfer To Paris Saint-Germain

Kylian Mbappe is one of the maximum talented footballers inside the global nowadays. He has already completed a lot in his younger career, together with triumphing the FIFA World Cup with France in 2018. However, his transfer to Paris Saint-Germain (PSG) in 2017 become a defining moment in his profession and marked the start of a brand new financial ruin in his life. In this essay, we will discover Mbappe's transfer to PSG, the impact it had on his career, and what it approach for the destiny of football.

Mbappe's switch to PSG became one of the maximum talked-about events inside the football global in 2017. The more youthful Frenchman had already mounted himself as one of the maximum promising game enthusiasts in Europe, having helped AS Monaco win the Ligue 1 choose out and acquire the semi-finals of the UEFA

Champions League. His performances had stuck the eye of an entire lot of Europe's pinnacle golf equipment, along with Real Madrid, Barcelona, and Manchester City.

However, it changed into PSG who acquired the race to sign Mbappe. The Parisian club had already spent a document-breaking €222 million to sign Neymar from Barcelona in advance that summer season, and they had been decided to characteristic Mbappe to their squad as nicely. The deal changed into ultimately agreed upon for a charge of spherical €one hundred 80 million, making Mbappe the second one-most expensive participant in records at the time, at the back of fine Neymar.

The switch modified into a big 2d in Mbappe's career. He modified into turning into a member of one in all the most crucial clubs in Europe, with a rich data and a passionate fan base. He become also joining a group that turn out to be decided to win the UEFA Champions League, having fallen brief in previous seasons irrespective of their domestic dominance.

For Mbappe, the waft to PSG represented a today's assignment. He turned into leaving in the back of the consolation and familiarity of AS Monaco, wherein he had grown up and superior as a player. He come to be additionally becoming a member of a set that had a wealth of facts, which consist of Neymar, Edinson Cavani, and Angel Di Maria. Mbappe would ought to combat for his area inside the organisation and show himself at the best level.

Mbappe's impact on PSG become immediately. He made his debut for the club in September 2017, scoring on his first appearance in a five-1 victory over Metz. He speedy installation himself as a key participant for the crew, forming a deadly attacking trio with Neymar and Cavani. Mbappe's tempo, capability, and finishing functionality made him a nightmare for opposition defenders, and he helped PSG win their home league name effortlessly.

However, it have become inside the UEFA Champions League in which Mbappe in reality shone. He scored four dreams in 8 appearances as PSG reached the Round of 16, collectively with a lovely brace closer to Bayern Munich in the organization stage. Mbappe's performances in Europe's excellent club opposition have been a easy indication of his capability and marked him out as one of the fine younger gamers within the international.

Mbappe's achievement at PSG grow to be not without its worrying situations, but. He confronted complaint from some quarters for his perceived loss of artwork rate and protecting contribution. He moreover had to take care of the strain of gambling for taken into consideration taken into consideration one among the largest golf equipment in Europe and the expectancies that got here with it. Despite the ones demanding conditions, Mbappe remained centered on his endeavor and endured to paintings hard on his weaknesses.

One of Mbappe's defining moments at PSG got here inside the 2019-20 season. He scored a lovable hat-trick inside the 2nd leg of PSG's Round of 16 tie in opposition to Borussia Dortmund, supporting the group overturn a 2-1 deficit and development to the region-finals. Mbappe's performance became a clear indication of his capabilities and his capability to carry out under pressure.

Mbappe's switch to PSG changed into furthermore big for the future of football. It marked a shift in power from traditional footballing giants like Real Madrid and Barcelona to clubs with first-rate financial assets, like PSG and Manchester City. The transfer costs worried in Mbappe's go with the flow had been first rate, and that they raised questions about the sustainability of such spending in the long term.

However, Mbappe's transfer additionally highlighted the significance of making an investment in young information. Mbappe become just 18 years antique even as he joined PSG, however he had already set up himself as one of the splendid game enthusiasts in Europe. His capability modified into smooth for all to see, and PSG were inclined to invest closely in him to strong his offerings.

Mbappe's success at PSG has moreover had an effect on French football. He has turn out to be a role version for younger French gamers, inspiring them to just accept as actual with that they will obtain their desires and reap the exceptional levels of the game. His performances for France in the 2018 World Cup were a easy indication of his abilties and his potential to emerge as one of the quality game enthusiasts of all time.

Mbappe's switch to PSG has had a huge impact on his profession and at the destiny of soccer. It marked a contemporary day bankruptcy in his existence and supplied him with new annoying conditions and opportunities. Mbappe has risen to the ones demanding situations, installing himself as one of the fantastic players within the international and scary a new era of footballers.

Kylian Mbappe's transfer to Paris Saint-Germain in 2017 changed into a defining moment in his profession. It marked a brand new economic catastrophe in his life and furnished him with new stressful conditions and opportunities. Mbappe has risen to those traumatic conditions, setting up himself as one of the exceptional gamers inside the worldwide and provoking a modern-day-day era of footballers. His achievement at PSG has additionally had an effect at the destiny of soccer, highlighting the importance of creating an funding in younger know-how and raising questions about the sustainability of such spending inside the long time. Mbappe's tale is an idea to more youthful footballers round the sector, and his effect on the game might be felt for many years to go back.

Chapter 16: Mbappe's Impact On The Football World

Ever because of the fact he burst onto the scene as a teenager, Mbappe has been hailed as one of the maximum gifted game enthusiasts of his generation, and he has in truth lived as a good deal as that billing. In this essay, we are able to discover Mbappe's effect on the soccer international, from his rise to stardom to his current-day reputation as an unstoppable stress on the pitch.

Mbappe's meteoric upward thrust to stardom started out out in earnest in a few unspecified time inside the destiny of the 2016-17 season, even as he burst onto the scene as a youngster gambling for AS Monaco. It became easy from the start that Mbappe have become a unique expertise, proudly owning an first rate combination of speed, functionality, and composure in the front of aim. He brief have become a key player for Monaco, helping them win the

Ligue 1 name and reach the semi-finals of the UEFA Champions League.

It have become all through that Champions League advertising campaign that Mbappe simply brought himself to the arena. He scored in every legs of Monaco's vicinity-very last tie in opposition to Borussia Dortmund, collectively with a cute purpose within the 2nd leg that showcased his awesome tempo and completing capability. That aim changed right into a clean indication of Mbappe's ability, and it became no wonder at the same time as the maximum important golf equipment in Europe came calling.

In 2017, Mbappe made a flow that might change the course of his career, signing for Paris Saint-Germain (PSG) in a deal actually worth round €100 and 80 million. The switch charge was a file on the time, and it marked Mbappe out as one of the most high priced gamers in records. However, it changed right right into a circulate that made sense for both Mbappe and PSG.

For Mbappe, the flow into represented a modern assignment and an possibility to play for one the diverse maximum vital clubs inside the worldwide. He become turning into a member of a team that changed into determined to win the UEFA Champions League, and he can be playing alongside some of the superb gamers inside the global, which encompass Neymar and Edinson Cavani. For PSG, the signing of Mbappe have grow to be a declaration of motive, a signal that they have been critical about competing with the most crucial clubs in Europe.

Mbappe's impact on PSG modified into right away. He scored on his debut for the club and speedy installation himself as a key player within the group. His speed and knowledge made him a nightmare for opposition defenders, and he unique a deadly attacking trio with Neymar and

Cavani. Mbappe helped PSG win their domestic league understand clearly, scoring thirteen desires in 27 appearances.

However, it grow to be inside the UEFA Champions League wherein Mbappe virtually shone. He scored four dreams in eight appearances as PSG reached the Round of 16, at the side of a adorable brace closer to Bayern Munich within the group degree. Mbappe's performances in Europe's most attractive membership competition have been a clean indication of his understanding and his ability to become one of the pleasant game enthusiasts in the international.

Mbappe's achievement at PSG has no longer been with out its challenges, but. He has faced complaint from some quarters for his perceived lack of paintings rate and defensive contribution. He has moreover needed to deal with the strain of gambling for one in each of the largest golf equipment in Europe and the expectancies that encompass it. Despite the ones demanding situations, Mbappe has remained centered on his endeavor and endured to art work tough on his weaknesses.

One of Mbappe's defining moments at PSG came within the 2019-20 season. He scored a lovely hat-trick inside the second leg of PSG's Round of sixteen tie closer to Borussia Dortmund, supporting the team overturn a 2-1 deficit and improvement to the place-finals. Mbappe's standard performance have become a easy indication of his expertise and his capability to carry out underneath strain.

Mbappe's impact on the football international extends past his performances on the pitch, however. He has turn out to be a role model for young players spherical the arena, inspiring them to bear in mind that they also can achieve greatness. Mbappe's achievement at this sort of more youthful age is a easy indication of what can be completed with tough art work and determination, and he has set a modern day huge for more youthful gamers to aspire to.

Mbappe's effect on French soccer has moreover been large. He has grow to be a image of desire for a modern generation of French gamers, inspiring them to consider that they can also accumulate achievement at the first-rate stage of the sport. Mbappe's performances for France in the 2018 World Cup have been a clear indication of his skills and his potential to turn out to be one of the best game enthusiasts of all time.

Mbappe's achievement at PSG has moreover had an impact on the future of soccer. His switch to PSG marked a shift in energy from traditional footballing giants like Real Madrid and Barcelona to clubs with giant monetary assets, like PSG and Manchester City. The transfer expenses involved in Mbappe's move had been first-rate, and they raised questions about the sustainability of such spending inside the long term.

However, Mbappe's switch moreover highlighted the significance of making an investment in greater younger expertise. Mbappe changed into truly 18 years antique at the same time as he joined PSG, but he had already installed himself as one of the excellent game enthusiasts in Europe. His ability changed into clean for all to appearance, and PSG were inclined to make investments heavily in him to regular his offerings.

Mbappe's achievement at PSG has additionally highlighted the significance of teamwork and collaboration. While Mbappe is surely one of the splendid gamers within the international, he can not reap success by myself. He is based totally on his teammates to create opportunities for him and provide him with assist at the pitch. Mbappe's fulfillment is a testomony to the significance of operating together within the route of a commonplace goal.

Looking to the future, Mbappe's effect at the soccer worldwide is about to hold. He remains in reality 22 years antique, and he has some years ahead of him to retain to extend and beautify. Mbappe has already achieved a lot in his younger profession, however there can be no question that he has the capacity to acquire even greater.

Kylian Mbappe is an unstoppable strain on the football pitch, a participant who has taken the location through the use of typhoon together with his high-quality talents and his functionality to score goals reputedly at will. His upward push to stardom has been not some component short of top notch, and his impact at the football global has been enormous. Mbappe's fulfillment at PSG has highlighted the importance of investing in greater younger capabilities and going for walks collectively in the path of a common aim. He has grow to be a role version for more youthful game enthusiasts around the arena, inspiring them to just accept as actual with that they also can benefit greatness. Mbappe's effect on the soccer worldwide is prepared to keep for decades to come lower back, and he's in reality one of the maximum interesting game enthusiasts to check in the game these days.

Chapter 17: Mbappe's Philanthropy And Personal Life

Kylian Mbappe isn't handiest a international-beauty footballer but moreover a philanthropist and a family guy. Off the pitch, he has used his popularity and fortune to make a pleasant impact on society and to encourage others to do the identical. In this essay, we're able to discover Mbappe's philanthropic efforts and private lifestyles, alongside alongside with his relationships, pursuits, and hobbies.

Mbappe's philanthropic work has been an critical a part of his life for the reason that he have become a professional footballer. He has used his platform to raise consciousness of severa social problems and to assist charities and foundations which can be close to his coronary coronary heart. One of the motives that Mbappe is specifically obsessed with is the combat in competition to youth poverty.

In 2018, Mbappe launched the "Inspired by means of way of KM" campaign, which aimed to elevate budget for Premiers de Cordée, a charity that permits children with disabilities take part in sports activities sports. The advertising campaign emerge as a massive fulfillment, raising over €500,000 in only some months. Mbappe moreover donated his whole World Cup bonus of €500,000 to the charity.

Mbappe's determination to preventing adolescents poverty extends beyond his charitable paintings. In 2019, he have grow to be an envoy for the charity Secours Populaire Français, which offers beneficial resource and resource to households in need. Mbappe has considerably applied his social media systems to raise awareness of the hassle, sharing snap shots and reminiscences of kids who are stricken by poverty.

Mbappe's philanthropic art work has not lengthy long past ignored. In 2020, he changed into named as honestly certainly one of Time mag's a hundred most influential people within the worldwide. The mag praised Mbappe for the use of his "prodigious know-how" to "convey preference to deprived youngsters."

Aside from his philanthropic artwork, Mbappe is likewise a dedicated family man. He is in an extended-term courting with Alicia Aylies, a former Miss France winner. The couple has been collectively whilst you do not forget that 2018 and has been noticed collectively at severa activities and on excursion.

Mbappe is likewise a doting father to his son, who became born in 2017. Despite his busy schedule, Mbappe makes time for his family and often stocks photos of them on his social media money owed. In an interview with L'Equipe, Mbappe spoke about the significance of own family in his lifestyles, pronouncing, "Family is the most important problem. They are normally there for me, and I am constantly there for them."

When he's not playing soccer or spending time together along along with his circle of relatives, Mbappe enjoys quite some pursuits and pursuits. One of his passions is style, and he has been observed sporting fashion dressmaker clothes and attending style suggests. Mbappe has moreover collaborated with apparel producers, consisting of Nike and Hugo Boss, to create his very personal clothing lines.

Mbappe is also a eager gamer and has been regarded to play FIFA and Call of Duty in his downtime. He even participated within the FIFA eWorld Cup in 2018, carrying out the arena-finals in advance than being knocked out.

In addition to his interests, Mbappe is likewise inquisitive about politics and contemporary-day affairs. He has spoken out on numerous troubles, on the aspect of racism in football and the refugee disaster. Mbappe has moreover expressed his admiration for former US President Barack Obama, announcing that he's a "outstanding instance" for more youthful humans.

Mbappe's personal existence and pastimes offer a glimpse into the person behind the footballer. He is a being worried and compassionate individual who makes use of his fulfillment to make a first rate effect on society. He is likewise a devoted own family man who values the significance of spending time with cherished ones. Mbappe's interests and hobbies show that he is a properly-rounded person with some of passions outside of football.

Kylian Mbappe's philanthropy and private lifestyles are simply as incredible as his performances on the football pitch. He has used his reputation and fortune to make a great impact on society, mainly inside the combat against teenagers poverty. Mbappe is likewise a devoted circle of relatives man who values the significance of spending time with loved ones. His hobbies and pursuits show that he's a nicely-rounded character with masses of passions out of doors of soccer. Mbappe's philanthropic paintings and personal lifestyles are a testomony to his individual and his willpower to developing the arena a better area.

MBAPPE'S LEGACY AND POTENTIAL

At simply 22 years vintage, Mbappe has finished greater than most footballers can dream of, collectively with prevailing the World Cup with France in 2018 and multiple domestic titles with Paris Saint-Germain. But what does the future preserve for this gifted young participant, and what is going to his legacy be inside the world of football?

Mbappe's meteoric upward push to recognition has been not some thing short of exceptional. He burst onto the scene as a teen at Monaco, in which he helped his crew win the Ligue 1 call and attain the semi-finals of the Champions League. His performances caught the attention of Paris Saint-Germain, who signed him for a international-report price of €a hundred and 80 million in 2017.

Since then, Mbappe has long gone from power to energy. He has received 3 consecutive Ligue 1 titles with PSG and has been a key participant in their run to the Champions League very last in 2020. Mbappe has moreover been a normal for the French country wide crew, assisting them win the World Cup in 2018 and achieving the very last of Euro 2020.

But what devices Mbappe other than one in every of a kind talented young gamers is his functionality. At definitely 22 years antique, he has already finished greater than most footballers do in their complete careers. However, there is however a lot greater to head again from Mbappe. He has all of the attributes to turn out to be one of the terrific footballers of all time, and his legacy in the sport may be vast.

One of Mbappe's finest strengths is his exceptional tempo. He is one of the fastest gamers in international football, and his pace is a ordinary chance to competition defenses. Mbappe's tempo permits him to get in at the back of defenses and create scoring opportunities for himself and his teammates. However, Mbappe is extra than best a pace merchant. He is also a absolutely proficient footballer with first rate technical functionality.

Mbappe's finishing is also a exquisite electricity. He has a scientific eye for purpose and is capable of scoring from a big kind of positions. Mbappe's finishing capability has been honed through years of practice and self-discipline, and it's miles one of the key reasons why he's this form of risky participant.

Another element of Mbappe's sport that units him aside is his mentality. Despite his young age, Mbappe has a adulthood and highbrow durability that belies his years. He is a confident player who prospers below stress and relishes the huge occasions. Mbappe's highbrow energy has been obvious at some point of his profession, specifically within the World Cup very last in 2018, where he scored a essential motive to help France win the event.

Mbappe's capacity isn't always most effective glaring on the pitch but furthermore off it. He is a characteristic model for younger humans round the arena, along together together with his charitable paintings and strength of will to social motives. Mbappe has used his platform as a professional footballer to raise cognizance of various social troubles, including youth poverty and the refugee catastrophe. He has also been concerned in severa charitable duties, which encompass the

"Inspired via KM" marketing marketing campaign, which raised finances for children with disabilities to take part in sports sports.

Mbappe's functionality off the pitch is in reality as mind-blowing as his capability on it. He has the ability to inspire a era of greater youthful people to make a brilliant impact on the arena and to use their abilties for correct. Mbappe's legacy is probably considered one in every of not quality a outstanding footballer but additionally a super humanitarian.

However, Mbappe's ability isn't always with out its annoying conditions. As he keeps to growth as a player, he will face growing pressure to perform at the first-class degree. The expectations located on Mbappe are massive, and he's going to need to keep to paintings difficult and stay centered if he's to satisfy them.

www.ingramcontent.com/pod-product-compliance
Lightning Source LLC
Chambersburg PA
CBHW070556010526
44118CB00012B/1338